# MONEY SKILLS FOR K PARENTS: A STEP-B GUIDE TO MANAGIN WISELY AND BUIL SMART FINANCIAL

RAISE FINANCIALLY INDEPENDENT K
DEBT TRAPS IN 7 SIMPLE, STRESS-F

KINGTHEROS PUBLIS

## TABLE OF CONTENTS

# INTRODUCTION

I started teaching my daughter before she even made her grand entrance into the world! Yep, I was that parent playing Mozart and talking to her while she was still cozy in her mom's belly. Even before saying "Mama," I became her personal encyclopedia. Numbers, colors, plants, languages, art—I threw it all her way. We explored everything from how to mix primary colors to how houses get built (yes, I dragged her to our house construction sites, hard hats and all). I was on a mission to raise a well-rounded mini-genius. But when it came to money... well, I hit a brick wall. I realized I had no idea how to teach her about it. So, naturally, I did what any parent would do—I became a student myself. And along the way, I figured out how to make learning about money fun for both of us!

It has become one of my passions to help families understand personal finance. I believe that teaching kids about money should start early and be fun. This book is my way of sharing what I've learned over the years, both from my professional experience and family life.

The truth is that financial education needs to be improved in many homes and schools. Many parents feel unprepared to teach their kids about money. Most kids grow up without understanding how to earn, save, spend, and invest wisely, which leads to financial scrabble later in life. But it doesn't have to be this way. With the proper guidance and tools, kids can grow up to be financially savvy adults.

The purpose of this book is simple: to provide a step-by-step guide for parents and kids on how to earn, save, spend, and invest money. This book will show practical ways to teach these skills and make them enjoyable for you and your kids. You'll find tips, activities, and stories to motivate everyone.

This book is for parents who want to help their kids develop good money habits. It's also for kids curious about money and want to learn how to manage it. Whether you're someone with experience, a financial novice, or just an educator who will instill financial responsibility in children, this book has something essential for you.

Here's what you can expect in the chapters ahead:

- **Chapter 1**: The Basics of Money - Understanding money and why it's essential.
- **Chapter 2**: Earning Money - From Allowance to Entrepreneurship
- **Chapter 3**: Saving and Budgeting: Building Financial Discipline.
- **Chapter 4**: Spending Money - Making intelligent spending choices and understanding needs vs. wants.
- **Chapter 5**: Investing Money: An introduction to investing and how it can grow your money over time.

- **Chapter 6**: Digital Financial Tools: Navigating the Modern World.
- **Chapter 7**: Credit and Debt: Understanding Borrowing.
- **A Heartfelt Conversation About Giving Back:** Philanthropy and Financial Responsibility

This book includes interactive activities like quizzes, charts, and games. These activities make learning about money fun and engaging, and you and your kids will enjoy working through them together.

My vision for this book is to see kids grow up with a solid understanding of personal finance. I want them to feel confident and capable of managing their money. The habits they develop now will serve them well throughout their lives.

So, let's get started on this financial journey together. By the end of this book, you and your kids will have the skills and knowledge to handle money wisely, setting them up for a successful financial future. Let's make learning about money a fun and rewarding experience for the whole family.

Are you ready? Let's dive in!

1

# THE BASICS OF MONEY: UNDERSTANDING MONEY AND WHY IT'S ESSENTIAL

## FOUNDATIONS OF FINANCIAL LITERACY

When my daughter asked me how many teeth she needed to leave under the pillow to buy a new video game console, I knew it was time for a family chat about money. Many kids and some adults don't understand how money works. That's okay, though—you're not alone. This chapter is here to clear things up. We'll cover the basics of money, its history, and why it's essential to understand. By the end, you'll know more about money than you ever thought possible.

### 1.1 UNDERSTANDING MONEY: WHAT IT IS AND HOW IT WORKS

Before coins and paper money, people used the **barter system**. This means that they traded goods and services directly. For example, if you had extra apples but needed some bread, you found someone who had bread and wanted apples. The barter system worked fine until someone didn't like your apples. Then, trading became tricky. That's where the money came in. Money made trading easier because everyone agreed on its value.

The first coins appeared around 600 BC in ancient Turkey. They made trading much easier because they were small, valuable, and easy to carry. Coins were made from metals like gold, silver, and bronze. Later, paper money was introduced. It first appeared in China around 600 AD and spread to Europe by the 1600s. Paper money was lighter than coins and more easily printed in large amounts.

In modern times, we also have **digital currency**. Digital currency includes things like Bitcoin and money stored in e-wallets. You don't see or touch this money, but it's real and can be used to buy things online. Digital money has made trading even more manageable, especially for online shopping.

Now, let's talk about how money is earned and circulated. People earn money by working jobs. This money is called a salary or wage. Once earned, money is often spent on goods and services. Goods are things you can touch, like food and clothes. Services are activities done for you, like haircuts or car repairs. Money spent on goods and services goes back into the economy. Businesses use this money to pay their workers, who then spend it again. This constant flow keeps the economy moving.

Banks and financial institutions play a significant role in this cycle. They keep money safe and lend it to others. When you put money in a savings account, the bank uses it to lend to others. The bank charges interest on these loans, which is how they make money. This interest is also how you earn a little extra on your savings. Banks offer many services to help people manage their money, like checking accounts and loans.

Understanding the value of money is also essential. The value of money is determined by how much people trust it and how much of it is available. Different countries have different currencies, like the US Dollar (USD), the Euro (EUR), and the Japanese Yen (JPY). The value of these currencies can change over time, which is called the exchange rate. For example, a dollar might be worth 100 yen one day, but the next day, it might be worth 110 yen. This change affects how much things cost when you travel or shop online from other countries.

Knowing how money works is crucial for several reasons:

1. It helps you manage your own money better. You'll know how to save, spend, and invest wisely.
2. It helps you avoid debt. Understanding money means you're less likely to borrow more than you can pay back.
3. It enables you to make informed decisions.

Whether buying a toy or saving for college, knowing how money works helps you make better choices.

**Financial independence** means you can manage your own money without always needing help from others. This freedom lets you make your own decisions and reach your financial goals. Avoiding debt is essential, but not all debt is bad. Debt happens when you borrow money and repay it with interest. Debt can help you buy a home, pay for education, or start a business if managed well. The key is borrowing only what you can afford and having a repayment plan. Good debt invests in your future; bad debt creates financial strain. Too much debt can cause stress and limit your financial freedom. Making informed decisions means knowing the risks and benefits of each choice. This knowledge helps you use your money wisely and achieve your goals.

So, understanding money is about more than just knowing its history or how it's made. It's about learning how to use it wisely. With this knowledge, you and your kids can make wise financial choices that will benefit you for life. Let's dive deeper into these concepts and see how you can apply them in your daily life.

## 1.2 THE IMPORTANCE OF SAVING: WHY SAVE MONEY?

Let's talk about saving money. Saving means setting aside some of your money instead of spending it immediately. Think of it as putting your money in a safe spot for future use. Imagine you want a new bike. If you spend all your allowance on candy, you won't have any left for the bike. But if you save some of that allowance each week, you'll eventually have enough to buy the bike without asking for extra money.

There are two main types of saving: short-term and long-term. Short-term savings are for immediate needs or emergencies. For example, if your pet gets sick, having some money saved up means you can help pay for the vet. Long-term savings are for bigger goals like education or retirement. It's like planting a tree that will grow over many years. You might need money for college or to buy a house one day. Starting to save now makes it easier to reach those big goals later.

Saving money has many benefits. One significant advantage is financial security. Having money saved up means you can handle unexpected expenses without stress. For example, if your computer breaks, you can use your savings to fix it instead of borrowing money. Another benefit is the ability to make larger purchases. With savings, you can buy things you want without relying on credit or loans. Savings also open up opportunities for a meaningful action: investing. Saving money enables you to invest it and grow your wealth over time.

There are different ways to save money. For younger kids, a **piggy bank** is a great start. It's a simple and fun way to see your savings grow. Each time you get money, put a part of it into the piggy bank. Opening a savings account at a bank is a good idea for older kids. Banks keep your money safe and pay you interest, which is extra money you earn to keep your savings there. Another effective method is using **saving jars**. You can designate different jars for specific goals, such as one for a new game and another for a school trip. This approach helps keep your savings organized and focused. However, my honest suggestion is to consider putting everything into high-yield savings accounts, whether saving for big future goals or an emergency fund. This way, you let your money work for you—"LM-MMM: Let the Money Make More Money." While your savings grow, you can still name the accounts based on your goals! As if they were in your jars.

Another more advanced strategy is to open a **Roth IRA** for minors. This is a powerful tool for long-term savings, allowing children or teenagers with earned income to start investing early in their future.

Real-life examples show how powerful saving can be. Take the story of a young entrepreneur who started selling homemade bracelets. She saved a portion of her earnings and invested in better materials. Her small business grew, and she could buy a new bike and save for college. Another example is a family saving for a vacation. They made a plan to save a little each month. By sticking to their plan, they had enough money for a fun trip without worrying about expenses.

Another excellent way for kids and adults to manage money effectively is using the **50-30-20 rule**. This budgeting method divides income into three simple categories: 50% for needs, 30% for wants, and 20% for savings and debt repayment. Needs include essentials like housing, food, and transportation, while the wants category covers discretionary spending like dining out or entertainment. The 20% designated for savings helps ensure that money's always set aside for future goals, such as retirement or building an emergency fund. This method promotes a healthy balance between living for today and preparing for tomorrow, making it a great financial strategy for the whole family.

You build a solid financial foundation by maintaining an emergency fund, opening a Roth IRA for minors, and following the 50-30-20 budgeting rule. These strategies help ensure you're prepared for future needs and equipped to handle unexpected challenges. They also encourage smart, long-term savings habits from an early age.

## 1.3 BUDGETING BASICS: SIMPLE TOOLS FOR KIDS

Imagine you get $10 every week for doing chores around the house. One week, you spend the whole $10 on apples - never on candies, they're not good for your health ;-). The following week, you want a new book but don't have any money left. This is where a budget can help. A budget is a plan for how you will spend and save your money. It enables you to ensure you have enough money for your needs and wants. A budget has two main parts: income and expenses. Income is the money you get, like your allowance. Expenses are the things you spend money on, like apples or books.

Balancing a budget means making sure your expenses don't exceed your income. If you get $10 a week, you can't spend more than $10, or you'll run out of money. This means you must choose what to buy and what to save for later. If you spend all your money on apples, you won't have any left for the book you want. But if you plan your spending, you can save some money each week and buy the book in a few weeks.

Let's introduce some simple budgeting tools that can help you manage your money. One great tool is a **budget worksheet**. This is a printable template where you can track your income and expenses. You write down how much money you get each week and what you spend on. It's like a money diary.

| | Projected cost | Actual cost | Difference |
|---|---|---|---|
| Mortgage or rent | $1,000 | $1,000 | $0 |
| Phone | $72 | $100 | ($28) |
| Electricity | $64 | $125 | ($61) |
| Gas | $35 | $35 | $0 |
| Water and sewer | $9 | $9 | $0 |

**Greenlight** is a great kid-friendly budgeting app. It allows kids to manage their virtual debit cards, set savings goals, and learn about budgeting in a fun and interactive way. Parents can also oversee transactions and add funds, making it a helpful tool for teaching financial literacy! These apps let you set savings goals and keep track of how much money you have saved and spent.

Tracking your income and expenses is essential. It helps you see where your money is going and how much you have left. You can start by recording your weekly allowance. Write down how much money you get each week. Then, keep a spending log. Every time you buy something, write it down. This helps you see how much you're spending on different things. You might be surprised to see how much you spend on candy or toys.

Sticking to a budget takes discipline, but it brings many benefits. It helps you avoid overspending and ensures you have enough money for the things you want. When you stick to a budget, you can save for bigger goals, like a new bike or a trip. Financial stability means you control your money, not vice versa. You're less likely to run out of money or need to borrow from others.

Another benefit of sticking to a budget is achieving goals. When you save money, you can reach your goals faster. Suppose you want to buy a new video game that costs $50. If you save $5 each week, you'll have enough money in 10 weeks. You can reach your goal without stress by sticking to your budget and saving a little each week.

| **Goal and cost** | **Weekly Allowance** | **Weekly Saved** | **Total Saved** | **Still need:** |
|---|---|---|---|---|
| Video Game: $50 | **10** | **5** | **5** | **45** |
| | | | | |
| | | | | |
| | | | | |

So, budgeting is like having a plan for your money. It helps you make smart choices and reach your goals, and you know what? It makes you stronger: it strengthens your self-discipline! By learning to budget, you become more mindful of your spending and can resist impulsive purchases. This way, you'll only buy what you truly need or can afford, making you a more informed and savvy shopper. You can manage your money like a pro with the right tools and a little discipline. Whether saving for a new toy or planning a big trip, a budget can help you get there. It's all about knowing how much you have and need and ensuring your expenses are within your income.

## 1.4 SPENDING WISELY: NEEDS VS. WANTS

Most of the time, when you tell kids you need to go over your expenses first, they look at you like you are speaking another language. Then, it's time to explain the difference between **needs** and **wants**. Needs are things you must have to live, like food, shelter, and clothing. These are basic necessities. With them, life gets pretty simple. Wants, on the other hand, are items that are nice to have but not necessary for survival. These include toys, video games, and that extra-large ice cream cone.

How do you decide what's more important to buy?

Is it okay to spend money on wants sometimes? Why?

Understanding the difference between Needs and Wants is the first step to spending wisely. Imagine you just got your allowance. Before you dash to the store to buy the latest toy, take a moment to think. Do you need it, or do you want it? Needs should always come first because they are essential for daily life. You can think about your wants once you've taken care of your needs. This helps you prioritize your spending and ensures you have enough money for the important stuff.

Creating a priority list can make this easier. Write down everything you need to spend money on and rank the list. Needs go at the top and Wants go at the bottom. If you have $10 and need $5 for lunch at school, then you have $5 to spend on Wants. You might want a toy that costs $6, but you only have $5 left. This is where trade-offs come in. You can save $5 this week and add it to next week's allowance to buy the toy. Or you could get a smaller toy that fits your budget. Making trade-offs helps you make wise spending decisions.

Practical tips can also help you spend wisely. One tip is to compare prices before buying something. Check different stores or websites to find the best deal. This way, you get the most value for your money. Another tip is to wait before making a purchase. If you see something you want, give yourself a day or two to think about it. This helps you avoid impulse buys, which are purchases made on the spur of the moment without much thought.

Let's look at a real-life scenario. Imagine you want a new video game that costs $40, but you only have $20 saved. You also want a new book that costs $10. You have to decide how to spend your money. You could buy the book now and save the rest for the game. Or you could save all your money this week and next week to buy the game. This decision-making process teaches you to think about your wants and make informed choices.

Another example is spending your allowance. Let's say you get $10 a week. You need $3 for school lunch, which leaves you with $7. You want a new toy, but you also need some new art supplies for a school project. By prioritizing, you can allocate $5 for the art supplies and save the remaining $2. This way, you meet your needs and still move closer to getting that toy later.

Wisely spending is all about making thoughtful choices. It helps you enjoy what you want while ensuring you have enough for what you need. With some planning and wise decisions, you can make your money go further and feel good about your spending.

## 1.5 INTRODUCTION TO EARNING: CHORES, ALLOWANCE, AND SMALL JOBS

Although one of my first "jobs" as a kid was helping a lady sell snacks on the beach, my friends earned their first money by doing chores around the house. Sweeping floors, washing dishes, and taking out the trash became their main gigs. In return, they got a weekly allowance, which felt like a mini paycheck. **Chores** are an excellent way for kids to start earning money. They teach responsibility and the value of hard work. Plus, it's nice to have a clean house! Making your bed, feeding the family pet, or mowing the lawn can earn you extra cash. Parents can decide how much to pay for each chore and how often. Weekly or monthly payments work well. This setup can help kids learn the basics of earning and managing money.

Now, let's talk about **allowances**. An allowance is money given regularly by parents to their kids. It's usually tied to completing chores or meeting certain expectations. Setting up an allowance system can teach financial responsibility. Parents, first, decide how much money to give and how often to give it. Weekly allowances work well because they provide regular practice in managing money. Kids, use this allowance to practice budgeting and saving. For example, you might save part of your allowance for a big purchase and spend the rest on smaller items. This helps you learn how to balance spending and saving.

**Entrepreneurship** is another exciting way to earn money. Starting your own small business can be both fun and rewarding. Think creatively about what you enjoy, like pet sitting, crafting, or lawn care, and how you can turn it into a business, and do some research to see if people in their community need that service. Lemonade stands are a classic example. You can also sell crafts, like homemade jewelry or artwork. To start a business, you can create a simple plan. Decide what you'll sell, how much to charge, and how to market your business. Budgeting is key. With minimal supplies and a system to track earnings and savings, kids can get started by spreading the word through friends, family, or social media (with parental help).

Success stories can be very inspiring. Take the story of a young girl who loved baking. She started selling her homemade cookies to neighbors and friends. She bought better baking supplies and expanded her business with the money she earned. Soon, she sold cookies at local events and made a nice profit. Another story is about a boy who started a lawn mowing business. He saved his earnings to buy better equipment and eventually hired his friends to help. His small business grew, and he learned valuable lessons about managing money and people.

Families with effective allowance strategies can also provide great examples. Some families create a **chore chart** with assigned payments for each task. This makes it clear what's expected and how much can be earned. Other families might match their kids' savings to encourage them to save more. For example, if you save $10, your parents might add another $10 to your savings. This motivates the kids to save and teaches them the value of money. I used to give bonuses to my daughter when I valued some excellent work in any area. Kids with decided goals prefer cash as a birthday present instead of any toy.

Earning money through chores, small jobs, or even starting a business can be a fun and educational experience. It teaches responsibility, time management, and financial skills. Whether you're washing dishes, babysitting, sweeping the floor, posing as a model, or selling lemonade, each experience helps you understand the value of work and money.

## 1.6 SETTING FINANCIAL GOALS: SHORT-TERM VS. LONG-TERM

Setting financial goals is like having a map for your money. It shows you where to go and how to get there. Without goals, it's easy to lose track of your money and find yourself wondering where it all went. Clear goals help you stay motivated. When you know what you're saving for, it's easier to stick to your budget and withstand the temptation to spend it on things you don't need. Goals also help with planning. They prepare you for future needs and desires. Whether buying a new bike or saving for college, having a plan makes it easier to get there.

There are **two types of goals**: short and long-term. **Short-term** goals are things you want to achieve soon. They might include saving for a toy, a trip, or a special treat. These goals are usually

achieved within a few weeks or months. **Long-term** goals take more time. They might include saving for college, a car, or even a house one day. These goals require more planning and patience because they take years to achieve. Both types of goals are important. Short-term goals keep you motivated and give you quick wins. Long-term goals help you plan for the future and are usually for long-lasting gratification.

To set realistic and achievable goals, use the **CLEAR method**. CLEAR stands for Concrete, Limited, Evident, Actionable, and Realistic. Concrete: Set a clear and detailed savings goal (e.g., saving for a vacation or an emergency fund). Limited: Define limits or constraints to keep the goal within reach (e.g., saving $100 monthly). Evident: Track visible progress (e.g., seeing your savings grow weekly or monthly). Actionable: Break the savings goal into manageable actions (e.g., automating transfers to your savings account). Realistic: Set a goal you can realistically achieve given your current financial situation (e.g., adjusting for your income and expenses). For example, "I want to save $50 for a new game in three months" is a CLEAR goal.

Using **goal charts** can help you keep track of your progress. A goal chart is a visual tool to mark your progress as you move closer to your goal. It can be as simple as a piece of paper with boxes to check off or a colorful chart you hang on your wall. Seeing your progress can be truly motivating. It reminds you of how far you've come and how close you are to achieving your goal.

Let's look at some real-life examples. One young boy wanted a new skateboard. He decided to save $5 each week from his allowance. He made a goal chart and marked his progress every week. In ten weeks, he had saved $50 and bought his skateboard.

Another example is a family saving for a vacation. They decided to save a little each month. They made a chart with their savings goal and marked their progress. By the end of the year, they had enough money for a fun family trip.

Setting financial goals isn't just about saving money. It's also about working together as a family. Discuss your goals with your family and work on them together. You may want to save for a new TV or a family vacation. By working together, you can achieve your goals faster and enjoy the rewards as a family.

Whether for a personal or family goal, I'd put my money in a High-Yield Savings Account. Online banks are excellent for this. Not only will your savings grow with the amounts you add each week or month, but it will also earn through *compound interest.* This means that even small savings will grow faster as you earn interest on the money you deposit and the interest already earned. It's an intelligent way to reach your goals more quickly!

Financial goals provide a feeling of direction and purpose. They help you stay focused on what's important and make it easier to manage your money. Whether saving for something small like a toy or something big like college, setting clear goals makes it possible. Remember, the key is to be specific, track your progress, and stay motivated. With the right goals, you can achieve anything you set your mind to. So, grab a pen and paper and start setting your financial goals today. It's the first step to making your dreams come true.

# 2

# EARNING MONEY:

## FROM ALLOWANCE TO ENTREPRENEURSHIP

When I was a kid, I always wanted a shiny new bike. My mother said I could earn it by doing chores around the house. I remember thinking, "How many dishes do I need to wash for this bike? Phew, sounded like too many dishes for one bike." That's when I first learned the value of hard work and earning money. This chapter is about helping you and your kids understand how chores and small jobs can teach valuable lessons about earning money.

### 2.1 CREATING A CHORE CHART: EARNING YOUR ALLOWANCE

Chore charts are like magic. They help kids understand the value of work and earning money. When you complete household tasks regularly, you learn responsibility. You know that it piles up if you don't take out the trash. Or if you don't feed the dog, he gets starving and gives you those sad puppy eyes. Doing chores teaches you that your actions matter. You see the results of your work, and that feels good.

Time management is another significant benefit. Kids often juggle school, homework, and playtime. Adding chores to the mix teaches you to allocate time for different tasks. You could wash the dishes right after dinner before settling down for some TV. Or you clean your room on Saturday morning so you can enjoy the rest of the weekend. Learning to balance chores with other activities is a skill that will help you throughout life.

Setting up a chore chart is easy and fun. Parents may start by making a list of age-appropriate tasks. Younger kids can handle simple chores like picking up toys or dusting. Older kids can take on more challenging tasks like vacuuming or mowing the lawn. Next, decide how often each chore should be done. Some chores, like feeding pets, are daily. Others, like taking out the trash, might be weekly. Finally, assign a monetary value to each chore. Washing the dishes earns them $1, while mowing the lawn earns them $5. This reward system helps kids understand that hard work pays off.

In today's digital age, chore chart apps are a fantastic tool to manage and track chores—apps like **Cozi Family Organizer**. While primarily a family calendar app, Cozi includes a chore chart feature. Families can assign tasks, keep track of progress, and manage schedules all in one place. **Child Reward** motivates kids with fun chores and rewards. A user-friendly chore tracker and reward system created to encourage children to complete their chores while instilling a sense of responsibility and the importance of hard work. With Child Reward, parents can effortlessly organize tasks, monitor progress, and reward their kids for their efforts and achievements. These apps help keep everyone organized and motivated.

Real-life examples show how effective chore charts can be. One family I know uses a colorful chart on their fridge. Each child has a list of chores and gets a sticker for every task completed. When they collect a certain number of stickers, they get to choose a reward. Another family uses an app to manage chores. The kids love checking off tasks on their tablets and seeing their earnings add up. They even have a family chore day once a week where everyone pitches in to tackle big tasks together.

Here's an interactive element for you to try at home:

**Create Your Chore Chart**

1. List of Chores: Write down all the chores around the house. Please make sure they are age-appropriate.
2. Frequency: Decide how often each chore should be done (daily, weekly, monthly).
3. Reward System: Assign a monetary value or reward for each chore.
4. Chart: Create a chart on paper or use an app to track the chores.
5. Stick to It: Follow through and reward the completed chores.

Using a chore chart helps keep the house clean and teaches valuable lessons about responsibility, time management, and the value of work. Whether you use a traditional paper chart or a modern app, the key is consistency and making it fun. So grab some markers, make a list, and, parents and kids, start working on those allowances to earn!

## 2.2 STARTING A SMALL BUSINESS: KID-FRIENDLY BUSINESS IDEAS

When I was a kid, I dreamed of starting my own business. I wanted to be my boss, make my own money, and finally have the power to say, "I'll have a cookie before dinner!" If you feel the same way, you're in luck! There are lots of simple and creative business ideas that are perfect for kids. The most classic idea is the **lemonade stand**. Setting up a lemonade stand is a fun way to earn money. You only need a table, cups, lemons, sugar, and water. Find a busy spot in your neighborhood and start selling. People love a refreshing drink on a hot day, and you'll love seeing your earnings grow.

But there are other ways to earn money beyond chores and lemonade stands. **Babysitting** is a popular job for older kids. Watching younger siblings or neighbors' kids can be both fun and profitable. **Pet sitting** is another option. If you love animals, you can offer to take care of pets when their owners are away. Make sure to be responsible and always keep the dogs safe. **Tutoring** is another fantastic business idea. If you're good at a particular subject, you can help younger kids with schoolwork. I have a friend who was a volleyball player as a kid, and now she tutors in that field. This enables you to earn money and reinforces your knowledge. Plus, it feels great to help others succeed. Then there's **lawn mowing**. I always considered buying my mower and presenting my services to my neighbors. Many people are willing to pay for help with their yard work. **Washing cars** for family, friends, or neighbors. Creating **handmade items** like bracelets, paintings, or DIY crafts to sell at local markets or online (with parental help). **Collecting and recycling** bottles, cans, or scrap materials for money. Doing **small tasks** like organizing, running errands, or cleaning for people in the community. **Taking photos** at local events, family gatherings, or for personal projects. Organizing a **garage sale** or selling old toys, books, or clothes online with help from parents. **Delivering newspapers**, flyers, or other small items for local businesses and **baking** cookies, cakes, or other treats to sell to friends and neighbors.

Online opportunities are growing in popularity, too. With the internet, there are many safe ways for kids to earn money online. For instance, you can **take surveys** or even sell handmade crafts on platforms like **Etsy**. **Assisting older people** or those less tech-savvy with setting up devices, social media, or apps. With parental guidance, kids can create a **YouTube channel**, blog, or social media presence around a hobby or skill and earn money through ads or sponsorships. Always get parents' approval and guidance when engaging in online activities. They can help you stay safe and find the best opportunities that match your interests and skills.

These small jobs can teach you how to manage your time and responsibilities and entrepreneurial skills. They also give you a taste of what it's like to have a real job while providing a fun way to earn money.

Starting a small business involves a few essential steps. First, you need to do some **market research**. This means determining if your community has a demand for your product or service. For example, if you want to start a lemonade stand, check for other stands in your area. If there are, think about what makes your lemonade unique. Maybe you use a secret recipe or offer a variety of flavors.

Next, you need to **set your prices**. Make sure your prices are fair and competitive. If you charge too much, people might not buy from you. If you charge too little, you might not make enough money to cover your costs. A good rule of thumb is to consider the cost of your materials and add extra for your time and effort.

**Marketing** is another crucial step. Let people know about your business. Marketing can be as simple as making posters or telling friends and family about your business. You can create flyers and banners and spread them in your neighborhood. Word-of-mouth is also powerful. Tell your friends and family about your business and ask them to spread the word. The more people know about your business, the more customers you'll get.

Running a business requires good **customer service**. Always treat your customers well. Be polite, friendly, and helpful. Happy customers are likelier to come back and tell others about your business. Time management is also crucial. Balancing your business with school and other activities can be challenging. Make a schedule and stick to it. Allocate specific times for your business tasks and ensure that you do not neglect your schoolwork.

Parents: Celebrating small successes—like making their first sale or hitting a savings goal—helps them stay motivated and develop essential life skills like responsibility, money management, and creativity.

**Financial tracking** is essential, too. Keep records of your income and expenses. This helps you see how much money you're making and where you can improve. Use a simple notebook or a spreadsheet to track your finances.

Let's look at some real-life examples of kid entrepreneurs. Riley Kinnane-Petersen started a jewelry business called Gunner & Lux when she was 13. Her business became so successful that big stores like Nordstrom and J.Crew started carrying her jewelry. Another inspiring story is that of Oliver "Ollie" Fequiere. At 9, he began Fizzies & Fables, a bath and story time business. He's involved in every process step, from ideas to product testing. Others like Moziah Bridges, who started his own bow tie business at the age of 9; Maya Penn, at just eight years old, launched her eco-friendly fashion line; Alina Morse created a line of sugar-free lollipops to promote dental health when she was just seven years old.

These young entrepreneurs show that age is just a number. You can start and grow a successful business with creativity, hard work, and determination. Remember, it's not just about making money. It's also about learning new skills, helping others, and having fun. So think of a business idea that excites you, and get started!

## 2.3 MAKING MONEY ONLINE: SAFE AND SIMPLE METHODS

The internet offers many ways to make money, even for kids. A straightforward way is by participating in **online surveys**. Some websites pay for your opinions on different topics. These surveys are usually short and easy to complete. Make sure the surveys are age-appropriate and safe. Another fun option is **content creation**. You can start a YouTube channel or a blog. Share your hobbies, teach something you know, or discuss topics you love. It's a great way to express yourself and earn some money through ads or sponsorships.

**Selling handmade items** is another excellent online opportunity. Platforms like Etsy allow you to sell crafts, from homemade jewelry to DIY decorations. If you enjoy making things, this could be a fun way to earn money. Imagine creating beautiful bracelets or cool custom t-shirts and selling them to people worldwide. The internet opens up a broad market for your creations.

**Game Streaming** or Esports (Twitch, YouTube): You may also make money by streaming yourself, playing video games, participating in tournaments, or creating gaming-related content. However, this requires parental guidance for safety.

**Print-on-Demand Stores** (Teespring, Redbubble): You can also design t-shirts, mugs, and other products with your artwork or slogans and sell them without handling inventory.

**Writing Blogs or eBooks**: You can start blogs on topics you love or write eBooks and sell them through platforms like Amazon Kindle. Writing lets kids share knowledge or stories while earning money through ad revenue or sales.

**Virtual Tutoring or Online Courses** (Outschool): Older kids passionate about teaching can share skills like math, art, or coding through virtual tutoring or creating courses. Platforms like Outschool allow kids to develop paid classes in areas of expertise.

While making money online is exciting, safety is essential. Always involve your parents in your online activities. They can help you navigate the internet safely. Set up privacy settings on your accounts to protect your personal information. Make sure only people you trust can see your details. Safe communication is crucial, too. Avoid talking to strangers online. Tell your parents immediately if someone you don't know tries to contact you. They can help you decide the best course of action.

Setting up online accounts might seem tricky, but it's straightforward with some guidance. For example, you must be 18 to have a PayPal account. However, you can use your parents' account with their permission. This way, you can receive payments safely. If you want to start a YouTube channel, YouTube Kids is a great place to begin. It's designed to be safe and kid-friendly, and your parents can help monitor the content and interactions.

Success in online ventures comes with consistency. If you start a YouTube channel or blog, post regularly. Your audience will expect new content; keeping a schedule helps grow your following. Captivate your audience by responding to comments and feedback. This makes your viewers feel valued and keeps them coming back. Focus on quality over quantity. It's better to have fewer high-quality videos or blog posts than many low-effort ones. People appreciate well-made content and are more likely to share it with others.

Imagine you love making slime. You start a YouTube channel showing how to make different types of slime. You post new videos every week and reply to comments from your viewers. Over time, your channel grows, and you start earning money from ads. Or you may enjoy painting. You set up an Etsy shop to sell your artwork. Each piece is unique, and you package and ship them nicely. Your customers leave great reviews, and more people start buying your paintings. These examples show how dedication and quality can lead to success online.

Making money online can be a stimulating adventure. Whether you're taking surveys, creating content, or selling crafts, there are many opportunities to explore. Stay safe, involve your parents, and focus on quality and consistency. You can turn your online activities into a profitable venture with the right approach.

## 2.4 BABYSITTING AND PET SITTING: RESPONSIBILITIES AND REWARDS

Babysitting and pet sitting are great ways to earn money while learning essential skills. Both jobs have responsibilities that teach you a lot about caring for others. When you babysit, you're responsible for watching over children. This includes ensuring they're safe, playing with them, and entertaining them. You might also need to prepare simple meals, help with homework, and prepare them for bed. It's essential to be patient and attentive. Kids can be full of energy and need someone who can keep up with them while ensuring their safety.

Pet sitting involves taking care of animals. Your tasks include feeding pets, giving them fresh water, and making sure they get enough exercise. Playing with pets, walking dogs, and cleaning litter boxes, are also part of the job. Just like with babysitting, you need to be responsible and attentive. Animals can't tell you what they need, so you must pay close attention to their behavior and ensure they're happy and healthy.

Getting started with babysitting and pet sitting can be easy if you know where to look. Start by asking family, friends, and neighbors if they need help. They already know and trust you, making it easier to get your first job. You can also create flyers and put them up around your neighborhood. Make sure to include your contact information and the services you offer. Online platforms can be helpful, too. Join reputable job boards where people look for babysitters and pet sitters. Make sure to read reviews and choose safe, well-known sites.

The rewards and benefits of these jobs go beyond just earning money. Babysitting and pet sitting can be quite profitable, with average rates for babysitting around $10-$15 per hour and pet sitting around $15-$20 per visit. These jobs also help you develop essential skills. You learn responsibility by taking care of others. Patience is critical, especially when dealing with energetic kids or pets. Time management is another skill you'll master, as you'll need to balance these jobs with school and other activities. Building trust is also a huge benefit. When you do a good job, people will recommend you to others, and you'll gain a positive reputation in your community.

Safety is paramount in both babysitting and pet sitting. Always have a list of emergency contacts. This should include the parents' or pet owners' phone numbers, a nearby relative or neighbor, and emergency services. Knowing basic first aid can be very helpful. Consider taking a first aid course or getting certified. This will teach you how to handle minor injuries and emergencies. Make sure the environment is safe. In babysitting, ensure no sharp objects or dangerous items are within the children's reach. For pet sitting, ensure the pets can't escape or get into harmful situations.

Imagine you're babysitting for the first time. The parents leave you a list of emergency contacts and show you where the first aid kit is. They also give you a rundown of their child's bedtime routine. You play games, help with homework, and prepare a simple dinner. When it's bedtime, you read a story and tuck the child in. The parents come home to find everything in order and their child happy. They're impressed and recommend you to their friends. Soon, you have more babysitting jobs lined up.

Consider caring for a neighbor's dog in pet sitting. They show you how much food to give and where the leash is. You take the dog for walks, play fetch in the yard, and ensure it has fresh water. The neighbor returns to find their dog happy and well-cared for. They tell others about your excellent service, and you get more pet-sitting requests. Babysitting and pet sitting teach you valuable skills while providing a steady source of income. They're a great way to start earning money and gaining experience.

## 2.5 CRAFTING AND SELLING: TURNING HOBBIES INTO CASH

If you love making things, why not turn that hobby into cash? There are many popular crafts you can make and sell for profit. Handmade jewelry, like bracelets, necklaces, and earrings, is always a hit. People love unique and personalized accessories. If you enjoy working with your hands, try making DIY decorations. Homemade candles, paintings, and ornaments can brighten any room and make great gifts. Personalized items, like custom t-shirt designs, are also in demand. You can generate designs that reflect your style and sell them to friends, family, and even online.

Pricing your crafts can be tricky, but it's essential to get it right. Start by calculating the cost of materials and labor. For example, if you spend $5 on beads and string for a bracelet and it takes an hour to make, consider how much your time is worth. If your time is worth $10 an hour, the bracelet should cost at least $15. This way, you cover your costs and make a profit. When it comes to selling, there are many options. Local craft fairs are a great place to showcase your work. You can set up a booth and meet customers face-to-face. Online marketplaces like Etsy allow you to reach a wider audience. You can create a store, upload photos of your crafts, and start selling.

Marketing is critical to getting your crafts noticed. Use social media platforms like Facebook and Instagram to promote your work. Share photos and stories about your crafting process. This helps build a connection with your audience. Creating a brand is also important. Consider what makes your crafts unique and how you want to present them. A catchy name and a consistent style can help you stand out. Use hashtags and engage with your followers to grow your online presence.

Crafting and selling have many benefits:

1. It allows you to channel your creativity into productive activities. Making things with your hands can be relaxing and rewarding.

2. It provides financial gain. Turning your hobby into a business means you can earn money doing something you love.
3. It helps you develop valuable skills.

Running a small business teaches you about pricing, marketing, and customer service. These skills will be helpful in many areas of your life.

Let's look at some successful young crafters. Lily Harper started Lily Lou's Aromas when she was nine. She makes imaginative candles and scents, and her business has grown steadily. Her future goal is to own a warehouse and have her products in big stores. Another inspiring story is that of Austin Gill, who co-founded Frères Branchiaux with his brothers. They make and sell candles by hand, and big stores like Whole Foods and Macy's carry their products. Austin loves basketball and making candles, and he balances both passions successfully. Mikaila Ulmer, at just four years old, started her artistic and eco-conscious business, inspired by her grandmother's flaxseed lemonade recipe and a passion for saving. Asia Newson started her candle-making business at age 5, selling her hand-poured candles door to door in Detroit.

These young artists show that age isn't a barrier to success. You can turn your hobbies into a profitable venture with creativity, hard work, and a little business know-how. Whether making jewelry, candles, or custom t-shirts, the key is to start small, learn as you go, and have fun with it.

Imagine you create a unique line of handmade bracelets. You start by selling them to friends and family. They love your work and tell others about it. Soon, you have a small but loyal customer base. You decide to take it further and set up a booth at a local craft fair. People admire your bracelets, and you make several sales.

Encouraged by your success, you opened an Etsy store and started promoting your work on social media. Orders start coming in from different places, and you realize your hobby has become a thriving business.

Crafting and selling offer endless possibilities. Whether you want to make some extra money or dream of building a business, it all starts with your creativity. Embrace your passion, put in the effort, and watch your hobby grow into something unique.

**Bonus: Children employed by their parents**

When a business is owned or operated by a parent or legal guardian, they can employ their children at any age, as long as the work is non-hazardous and not restricted by law. The child can work any hours, provided the parent or guardian supervises them. This can be a great learning opportunity for kids to gain real-world business experience. Plus, for parents, employing their children can offer tax benefits, as they may be able to deduct the wages paid to their child as a business expense—making it a win-win for the family!

## 2.6 MAKING A BUSINESS PLAN: STEPS TO SUCCESS

Imagine you're setting up a lemonade stand. You wouldn't just throw a table outside and hope for the best, right? You'd plan how much lemonade to make, how much to charge, and where to set up. That's why having a business plan is so important. It's like a roadmap guiding your business towards its goals. Without it, you might get lost along the way. A good business plan helps you gain support from parents or investors. They'll see you have a solid plan and are serious about your idea. It also enables you to track progress. You can measure your achievements and make adjustments as needed.

A solid business plan has several vital components. First, the **executive summary** is a brief overview of your business. It explains what your business does and its goals. Next is the business description: you go into more detail about your business. What products or services do you offer? Who are your customers? What makes your business unique? Then comes the **market analysis**: this part helps you understand your target market and competition. Who are your customers? What do they need? Who else is offering similar products or services? Knowing this helps you stand out.

The **marketing strategy** is another crucial part: it explains how you'll attract and retain customers. Will you use flyers, social media, or word-of-mouth? How will you keep customers coming back? The **financial plan** is also essential: it includes your budget, pricing, and financial projections. How much will it cost to start your business? How much will you charge for your products or services? How much do you expect to make in the first few months?

Creating a business plan might seem daunting, but it doesn't have to be. There are many templates and examples available to help you get started. A simple business plan template can guide you through the process. It breaks down each section and provides prompts to help you think about your business. Sample business plans can also be helpful. They show you what a completed plan looks like and give you ideas for your own.

Here's a template to get you started:

1. Executive Summary: Briefly describe your business and its goals.

2. Business Description: Explain what your business does and what makes it unique.
3. Market Analysis: Analyze your target market and assess your competition.
4. Marketing Strategy: Plan how you'll attract and keep customers.
5. Financial Plan: Outline your budget, pricing, and financial projections.

Creating an effective business plan involves a few practical tips. First, let's have involved parents and children. When we did our first, even grandparents were involved. Adults can provide guidance and support. They might have experience or insights that can help you. Next, set realistic goals. Your goals should be achievable and measurable. For example, instead of saying, "I want to make a lot of money," say, "I want to make $50 in the first month." This gives you a clear target to aim for. Finally, review and revise your plan regularly. As your business grows, your plan might need updates. Regularly check your progress and make adjustments as needed.

Imagine you're starting a dog-walking business. You create a business plan with an executive summary, business description, market analysis, marketing strategy, and financial plan. You discuss your plan with your parents, who give you great advice. You set a goal to walk five dogs a week and make $50 in the first month. You use flyers and social media to promote your business. As you gain customers, you track your income and expenses. You review your plan regularly and make adjustments as needed.

Involving your parents can provide valuable insights and support. They might have experience in areas you need to become more familiar with. They can help you set realistic goals and track your progress. Setting goals that are achievable and measurable gives you something to work towards. It keeps you motivated and focused. Regularly reviewing and revising your plan ensures you stay on track. It allows you to make necessary adjustments and continue progressing.

Making a business plan might sound like a lot of work, but it's worth it. It helps you stay organized, gain support, and track your progress. Whether starting a lemonade stand, a dog-walking business, or any other venture, a business plan is crucial for success. So grab a pen and paper and start planning your business today. With a solid plan, you're well on your way to success.

Here's a fun and interactive activity designed for a single family to create a business plan together during a Finance Family Night. This activity introduces fundamental business concepts while encouraging creativity, teamwork, and practical problem-solving.

**Activity: "Start Your Family Business"**

**Objective:**

The family will work together to create a simple business plan for an imaginary business. By the end of the activity, they'll have designed a product or service, identified customers, and figured out how much they'll need to start their business and make a profit.

**Materials:**

- Business Plan Worksheet (a printout or simple template)
- Blank Paper for Brainstorming
- Markers, pens, pencils
- Supply Cards (index cards with ideas like "ingredients," "packaging," "website," "employees," etc.)
- Fake Money (to help with budget planning)

**How to Play:**

1. Introduction (5 minutes):
    - Start by explaining to the family what a business plan is in simple terms: "A business plan is like a roadmap that helps you figure out what you're going to sell, who's going to buy it, and how you're going to make money."
    - Highlight three key elements:
        - Product or Service (What are they selling?)
        - Target Market (Who will buy it?)
        - Budget/Costs (What will they spend, and how will they make a profit?)
2. Choose Your Business Idea (5 minutes):
    - The family brainstorms a fun business idea together. If they need inspiration, provide a few examples:
        - Lemonade Stand (selling lemonade)
        - Dog Walking Service (offering pet care)
        - Toy Design Shop (creating custom toys)
        - Craft Workshop (making and selling crafts)
    - Encourage everyone to contribute ideas and settle on one the family feels excited about.
3. Design the Business Plan (10 minutes):
    - Using the Business Plan Worksheet, the family will fill in key details about their business:
        - Business Name: Pick a catchy and creative name for the business.
        - Product or Service: What will they sell or offer? Be specific (e.g., lemonade with special flavors, custom pet collars).
        - Target Customers: Who will buy it? (e.g., kids, neighbors, pet owners)
        - Supplies Needed: Review the Supply Cards to

    determine what they'll need to run their business (e.g., ingredients, website, employees, equipment).
    - Business Goals: Set goals like how many products they'll sell or how much money they hope to make.

4. Budget Time (10 minutes):
    - The family will receive a set amount of fake money (e.g., $100) and must decide how to spend it on the items from their Supply Cards.
    - They'll discuss and prioritize spending on things like ingredients, advertising, and packaging. The goal is to determine how much they'll need to spend to get the business up and running and how much they plan to sell.
    - Use a simple "Profit = Sales - Costs" approach to determine how much they might make.
5. Create a Marketing Poster (10 minutes):
    - Let the family design a fun and colorful marketing poster to advertise their business.
    - The poster should include the business name, what they're selling, a slogan, and maybe a fun drawing of the product or service.
    - The family can get creative and make the poster look as fun or professional as possible.
6. Presentation (5 minutes):
    - The family presents their business plan to each other, explaining what they're selling, who will buy it, and how they plan to make a profit.
    - Encourage a lighthearted conversation about the process—what did everyone learn about teamwork, planning, and budgeting?

**Optional Bonus:**

- Fun Twist (5 minutes): Partway through, introduce a funny "challenge" to the plan to help the family think on their feet. For example, "Uh-oh, the lemonade stand ran out of lemons! How will you adjust your plan?"
- Family Voting: If possible, allow other family members (if available) to vote on the best part of the business plan, such as the most creative idea or the funniest twist.

**Takeaway:**

- After the activity, provide the family with a Simple Business Plan Template that they can fill out further at home or build on if they'd like to work on real business ideas together.

**Learning Outcomes:**

- Creativity & Innovation: Brainstorming a business idea encourages creative thinking.
- Basic Financial Literacy: Kids and parents learn about budgeting, costs, and profits.
- Teamwork: Working together fosters communication, cooperation, and family bonding.

This activity offers a fun, hands-on way to introduce kids and parents to the basics of business planning in a playful and engaging setting!

# 3

# SAVING AND BUDGETING:

## BUILDING FINANCIAL DISCIPLINE

As a kid, I had this massive jar for my coins—like it was *legendary*. Every time I tossed a coin in, it felt like I was adding to a treasure chest, even though it took forever to fill up. I'd watch it slowly climb, one lonely penny at a time, but man, that sense of accomplishment was *real*. That jar taught me the power of saving, one clink at a time. These days, piggy banks do the same thing. They help kids *see* their savings grow, turning the whole "save your money" idea into something more exciting—and maybe even fun!

### 3.1 THE POWER OF PIGGY BANKS: VISUALIZING SAVINGS

Piggy banks are essential tools for teaching children the value of saving money. Unlike digital displays, they offer a tangible way to track progress, making saving a concrete visual experience. This is particularly important for young savers, who benefit from seeing their money accumulate. There's a piggy bank for every personality. Classics are made from ceramic or plastic and come in various

designs, including animals and superheroes. Modern digital versions automatically count and display the amount saved as coins are inserted, providing instant feedback on your savings. For a personalized touch, DIY piggy banks made from everyday items like jars or boxes encourage creativity and ownership of the saving process. Selecting the ideal piggy bank involves considering size and accessibility for larger goals. Some are equipped with simple openings for easy access, while others are designed to be broken when complete, fostering discipline against impulsive spending.

Regular saving is a habit that pays off big time. Even small amounts add up over time. Setting a savings routine can help make this habit stick. For example, you may put money into your piggy bank every week or month. Consistency is key. Watching your piggy bank fill up week by week can be very motivating. It's like watching a garden grow. Every coin is a seed, and you'll see your savings bloom with patience.

**Goal-oriented saving** is another great way to stay motivated. Setting specific savings goals can help you focus and stay on track. For short-term goals, you may save for a toy, a book, or a fun outing. Long-term goals could include saving for something bigger, like a bicycle or trip. Having a clear goal makes saving more exciting. You know precisely what you're working towards, which makes it easier to stick to your plan.

To make saving even more fun, try creative ways to use your piggy bank. Decorating your piggy bank can be a great start. Use stickers, paint, or markers to personalize it. Make it as unique as you are. Another fun idea is to create savings challenges. Challenge yourself to save a certain amount by a specific date. You can even involve friends or family members in the challenge. Who can save the most in a month? Turn saving into a game; it won't feel like a chore.

You can also try the 3 Piggy Bank Method, which involves using three separate banks for spending, saving, and sharing. This method helps you allocate your money wisely. The spending bank is for fun, minor purchases like snacks or small toys. The savings bank is for bigger-ticket items like a deluxe Lego set or a scooter. The sharing bank is for charitable efforts, like supporting an animal shelter or providing books for school children. This method teaches you to balance your money and think about different ways to use it.

I *love* saving for something that's not just a cool gadget or the latest trend but something that will make you *more* money—like starting your own business. It's like planting a seed instead of just picking the fruit. Sure, buying something fun feels excellent, but imagine saving up to kickstart a business that lets you *keep earning* over and over again. That's next-level thinking!

Piggy banks are more than just containers for spare change. They are tools that teach you valuable lessons about saving, goal setting, and financial discipline. Whether you choose a traditional, digital, or DIY piggy bank, the key is to make saving a regular habit. Set your goals, decorate your piggy bank, and start a savings challenge. Each coin you save brings you one step closer to your goal.

**Bonus: Check-Off Challenge**

When my daughter was about three years old, we started using this method, and before we knew it, we had saved up enough to buy our first refrigerator. She was so proud, inspecting it like it was her very own treasure! That's the beauty of the Check-Off Challenge—it turns saving into a fun and strategic game. Every dollar saved brings you closer to your goal, making the process feel like an adventure rather than a chore. Here's how it works:

You start by listing numbers, typically from 1 to 100 (or any range you choose, depending on your savings goal). Each number on the list represents a dollar amount. So, if you list numbers from 1 to 100, you'll save anywhere from $1 to $100 at a time.

Here's the cool part: each time you save a specific amount, you check off the number that matches it. For example, if you put $1 in your savings jar or account, you check off the number 1. If you save $5, you check off number 5. You keep going until you've checked off every number on your list.

Now, why is this method excellent?

**1. Flexibility**

You don't have to save the same amount every week or month. In some weeks, you might only be able to save $1 or $2. That is fine; check off those numbers! On other weeks, you might feel like a high roller and save $50—go ahead, check off number 50. The flexibility allows you to save based on what you can afford at any given time.

**2. Built-in Motivation**

Each time you check off a number, you get a little satisfaction. It's like leveling up in a game or crossing something off a to-do list. The more numbers you check off, the closer you are to completing the challenge! You can see how quickly you can finish the list.

**3. Psychological Benefits**

This method plays on the psychological trick of *chunking*. Instead of focusing on saving a large sum all at once, you're breaking it down into smaller, manageable goals. Saving $100 might feel daunting initially, but saving $1, $2, or $7 at a time is much more approachable. The small wins keep you motivated and push you to continue.

**4. Control Over Progress**

You can tailor your approach to fit your financial situation. You may want to knock out the higher numbers first to get them out of the way, or you'll start with the smaller numbers to build momentum. Either way, you control how quickly (or slowly) you want to complete your savings goal.

**5. The Power of Small Contributions**

Even though you save in small increments, those little amounts add up quickly. Let's say you complete the full list of numbers from 1 to 100. By checking off every single number, you will have saved $5,050! If you do this with higher numbers, say 1 to 200, you're looking at a hefty $20,100 saved once you're done. It's proof that consistent small efforts can lead to big results.

**6. Add Your Twist**

You can get creative with this method. For instance, you could save double the amount for each number or add bonus savings for specific numbers (like a "jackpot" number where you save extra). Some even make it a family or group challenge, where everyone checks off numbers and saves together.

**Example:**

If you're doing numbers from 1 to 100, you might save like this:

- Week 1: Save $1, check off #1
- Week 2: Save $20, check off #20
- Week 3: Save $5, check off #5

You get to pick and choose based on what's realistic for you at any given time. The ultimate goal is to check off *all* the numbers, and when you do, you'll have built up a nice little savings stash.

The method is simple, flexible, and effective. It turns saving money into a challenge that feels rewarding instead of like a chore. It never feels overwhelming because you're chipping away at the goal one step at a time.

In the end, you will not only have checked off all those numbers but also have built up a sense of achievement and discipline when it comes to saving money!

## 3.2 OPENING A SAVINGS ACCOUNT: WHAT KIDS AND PARENTS NEED TO KNOW

Opening a savings account is a big step towards learning about money. Unlike a piggy bank, a savings account helps your money grow over time through interest. Interest is the extra money the bank pays you to keep your money with them. It's like a reward for saving. When you deposit money into a savings account, the bank uses it for loans and other investments. In return, they give you a small percentage of that amount, called interest. Over time, this interest adds up, especially with compound interest, where you earn interest on your interest.

Safety and security are other big benefits of having a savings account. Banks are designed to keep your money safe. They have vaults, security systems, and insurance to protect your funds. Unlike money kept at home, which can be lost or stolen, money in a bank is much safer. Plus, having a savings account helps you learn about the banking system and how to manage your finances. It's a real-world experience that teaches valuable lessons.

Opening a savings account is easier than you think. First, you'll need some documents. You'll need identification, like a birth certificate or passport, and proof of address. Your parents will also need their ID and proof of address. Next, you'll need to choose a bank. Look for a bank that offers reasonable interest rates and low fees. Some banks even have special accounts for kids with extra perks like birthday bucks or educational apps.

Once you've chosen a bank, head to the branch with your documents, and a bank officer will help you fill out the necessary forms. They might ask for your Social Security number and other details. Make sure to ask about any fees or minimum balance requirements. Some banks charge fees if your balance drops below a certain amount; I avoid those accounts. Others offer free accounts for kids. Once everything is set up, you'll get your account details and maybe even a passbook or bank card.

Managing a savings account is the next step. You'll need to know how to deposit and withdraw money. You can deposit money by visiting the bank and handing it to a teller. They'll update your account balance. Some banks have ATMs where you can deposit cash or checks. Online banking is another option. With online banking, you can transfer money, check your balance, and even set up automatic transfers from your allowance to your savings account.

Keeping track of your account is crucial. Regularly monitor your account statements to see how much you've saved and how much interest you've earned. Most banks send monthly statements, either by mail or online. Reviewing these statements helps you stay on top of your finances. If you notice any errors, report them to the bank immediately.

Understanding **interest** is critical to making the most of your savings account. There are two types of interest: **simple** and **compound**. Simple interest is calculated on the principal amount, which is the initial amount you deposited. If you have $100 in your account and the bank offers a 5% simple interest rate, you'll earn $5 a year. Compound interest is more powerful. It's calculated on the principal and the accumulated interest. With compound interest, your money grows faster because you earn interest on your interest.

Interest rates vary between banks and account types. Higher interest rates mean more earnings. When choosing a savings account, look for one with competitive rates. Even a tiny difference in the interest rate can significantly impact the results over time. For example, an account with a 2% interest rate will grow faster than one with a 1% interest rate.

Opening a savings account is a smart move. It teaches you about money management, helps your savings grow, and keeps your money safe. It's a step towards financial independence and a valuable learning experience. So gather your documents, choose a bank, and take that vital step towards managing your money wisely.

## 3.3 ROTH IRA FOR MINORS

Opening a Roth IRA for minors is a more advanced, yet powerful, method of saving. It's an excellent opportunity for parents and kids to work together to build long-term financial security. With a Roth IRA, children or teenagers who have earned income can start investing early for their future. This allows their savings to grow tax-free over time, giving them a considerable head start on building wealth for retirement or other financial goals. Even though Roth IRAs are typically associated with adults, minors who earn income from part-time jobs, babysitting, or working in a family business can open a Roth IRA with the help of a parent or guardian. The child can contribute up to the lesser of their earned income or the annual contribution limit (currently $6,500 for 2024). One of the most significant benefits of a Roth IRA is that the money invested grows tax-free, and when the child reaches retirement age, withdrawals are also tax-free. Over time, the power of compound interest allows their savings to increase significantly. Additionally, the flexibility of Roth IRAs means that contributions (though not the earnings) can be withdrawn at any time without penalty, offering financial flexibility.

Imagine you have a particular savings account where you put $1,000 every year, like saving part of your allowance. But this isn't just any regular account—it grows approximately by 7% every year, like magic!

**After 10 Years:**

If you keep adding $1,000 yearly, your account could grow to $13,816! That's way more than you put in because your saved money keeps growing.

**After 20 Years:**

If you keep saving for 20 years, your account could grow to $40,995! The longer you leave it, the more it grows—just like planting a tree that grows yearly.

By saving regularly, you're letting your money work for you and grow into something much bigger!

Institutions like Fidelity, Charles Schwab, and Vanguard allow parents to open a custodial Roth IRA for minors. They are all trustworthy, have strong reputations, and offer a range of tools for both parents and children to learn and build wealth over time.

**Some key factors to consider:**

- No Account Minimums or Low Fees: Look for platforms with minimal costs to open and maintain the account.
- Investment Variety: Ensure access to various investment options, including index funds, ETFs, and individual stocks.
- Ease of Use: Choose a platform that is simple to navigate and offers good educational resources to teach kids about investing.
- Custodial Options: Roth IRAs for minors must be custodial, meaning a parent or guardian manages the account until the child reaches the age of majority.

## 3.4 ALLOWANCE BUDGETING: CREATING A WEEKLY PLAN

Budgeting an allowance might sound boring, but it's a powerful tool for building financial discipline. Think of it as a game where you decide how to use your money wisely. Budgeting helps you understand the difference between income and expenses. Income is the money you get, like your weekly allowance or any extra cash you earn from small jobs. Expenses are what you spend on things like snacks, toys, or saving for something bigger. Balancing these helps ensure you don't run out of money before you get more.

When you get your allowance, spending it all at once is tempting. But dividing it into categories can help you manage it better. You can allocate your money in different ways. For example, set aside part of it for immediate spending, another part for saving, and a tiny part for sharing or donating. This way, you cover your needs, work towards your goals, and practice generosity. Allocating funds helps you see where your money goes and makes it easier to stick to your budget.

Creating a weekly budget is simple and fun. First, list your income. Write down how much allowance you get each week and any other money you might earn. Then, think about your expenses. Make a list of things you need to spend money on. This could include school supplies, snacks, or saving for a new game. Now, allocate your money to each category. Decide how much to spend, how much to save, and how much to share. This way, you have a clear plan for your money.

Tracking your expenses is the next step. Each time you spend money, write it down. This helps you see where your money goes and if you're sticking to your budget. You can use a simple notebook or a digital tool to keep track. The key is to record every expense, no matter how small. This habit helps you stay on top of your finances and makes it easier to adjust if needed.

There are many tools you can use to create and manage your budget. **Budget worksheets** are a great start. These printable templates help you list your income and expenses and allocate your funds. You can find many free templates online. For a more tech-savvy approach, try budgeting apps. Apps like **Chores &**

**Allowance Bot** are designed for kids and make budgeting fun. These apps let you track your income and expenses, set savings goals, and assign chores for extra earnings. They're like having a digital money manager in your pocket.

Sticking to a budget can be challenging, but with some practical tips, you can do it. First, set your priorities. Focus on needs before wants. Ensure you have enough money for essential things like school supplies or saving for a big goal before spending on fun items. This helps you save money for things you really need. Second, regularly review and adjust your budget. Check your expenses and see if you're staying on track. If you're spending too much in one category, adjust your budget to balance it out. This keeps your finances in check and helps you make better decisions.

Sometimes, you might be tempted to spend more than planned. That's normal, but try to resist the urge. Remember your goals and why you're saving. If you do overspend, adjust your budget to make up for it. You could save a little less next week to cover the extra expense. The key is to stay flexible and keep your goals in mind. Budgeting is not about being perfect; it's about making smart choices and learning from your mistakes.

Allowance budgeting is a powerful tool that helps you manage your money, reach your goals, and build financial discipline. By understanding your income and expenses, allocating funds, and using simple tools, you can create a budget that works for you. Please stick to your budget, review it regularly, and adjust as needed. With practice, you'll become a budgeting pro.

**Interactive Budgeting Activity: "Family Budget Challenge"**

**Objective:**

Teach kids how to create and manage a budget by involving parents in a fun, hands-on activity. This challenge helps kids understand income, expenses, and savings through real-life examples, as well as teamwork with their parents.

**Materials:**

- A large piece of paper or poster board (or use a whiteboard)
- Colored markers
- Fake money or coins (you can use play money or cut paper into money shapes)
- Printouts or cards with everyday expenses (e.g., food, toys, utilities, entertainment, school supplies)
- A calculator
- Envelopes (optional)

**Steps:**

1. Set the Scene:

Explain to your kids that they will create a family budget for the month, just like a real family does! Introduce the idea of budgeting as a plan for using your money for different things like food, fun, and savings.

2. Identify Income:

Together, decide on a fictional income for the family. For example, you could say the family "earns" $1,000 for the month. Use fake money to make it more interactive. You can even let kids "earn" this money through simple chores, quizzes, or challenges during the activity to get them engaged.

3. List Expenses:

Create categories for monthly expenses:

- Needs: Rent/mortgage, food, utilities, transportation, etc.
- Wants: Toys, movies, dining out, games, etc.
- Savings: Emergency fund, future goals, etc.

Use cards with drawings or words to represent each category (e.g., a picture of a house for rent, a toy for fun expenses, etc.).

4. Allocate the Budget:

Give kids the $1,000 in fake money and go through each expense category. Ask them to "pay" for each expense by distributing the money among different categories:

- How much will go to rent?
- How much will they spend on toys and fun activities?
- How much do they want to save?

Let them physically hand over the play money for each category.

5. Introduce a Savings Goal:

Choose a family savings goal, such as saving for a trip, a new game, or an emergency fund. Work together to decide how much to allocate toward savings each month. Use envelopes or jars labeled for each savings goal, and let the kids put the saved money in there.

6. Unexpected Events:

Introduce "unexpected expenses" to add a twist to the activity. For example, pull a card that says, "The car broke down. You need

$200 to fix it!" or "Your friend's birthday party is this weekend; you need $50 for a gift."

Have the kids figure out how to adjust the budget to cover the surprise expense—do they dip into savings, cut back on fun activities, or find another solution?

7. Review & Discuss:

Once the budget is complete, review it together. Discuss whether they spent too much in certain areas, whether they saved enough, and how they handled the unexpected expenses. Discuss the importance of prioritizing needs over wants and always putting something into savings.

8. Challenge Extension (Optional):

Track your family's actual weekly or monthly spending for an ongoing challenge. Let the kids participate in the tracking, and then revisit your budget at the end to see how it compares to real-life spending.

**Reflection Questions:**

- What did you find most surprising about the budget?
- Was it hard to save money for unexpected expenses?
- How did it feel to set money aside for savings instead of spending it all on fun things?
- What would you do differently next time?

This activity makes budgeting fun and helps kids grasp the importance of managing money, setting goals, and being prepared for surprises. By working with parents, they learn valuable life skills while feeling empowered to contribute to family decisions!

## 3.5 SAVING FOR BIG GOALS: HOW TO PLAN AND ACHIEVE

Setting big financial goals is like dreaming about the future. It gives you something exciting to work towards and keeps you motivated. Whether saving for a bicycle, a family trip, or even college, having long-term goals helps you stay focused. These goals teach you the importance of planning for the future. They show you that big dreams are possible with patience and effort. When you save for something big, you learn to appreciate the value of hard work and persistence.

One of the best ways to achieve big goals is to break them down into smaller steps. This makes the process less overwhelming and more manageable. Think of it like building a tower with blocks. You don't just stack all the blocks at once. You do it one block at a time. The same applies to saving money. Start by setting **milestones**, which are intermediate targets along the way. For example, if you aim to save $100, set milestones at $25, $50, and $75. Each milestone is a small victory that brings you closer to your big goal.

Creating a **timeline** is another helpful strategy. Plan when you want to achieve each milestone. This could be weekly, monthly, or even quarterly. Having a timeline keeps you on track and helps you see your progress. It also makes the goal more concrete. Instead of saying, "I want to save $100," you say, "I want to save $25 by the end of this month." This specific timeline makes your goal feel more achievable.

When creating a savings plan, start by calculating the total cost of what you want. If you're saving for a bicycle that costs $200, that's your target amount. Next, determine how much you can save each week or month. If you get a weekly allowance of $10, decide how much you can set aside. You could save $5 each week. This means it will take you 40 weeks to reach your goal. Breaking it down in this way makes the big number seem less intimidating.

Let's look at some real-life examples to inspire you. Imagine you want to save for a new bicycle. First, calculate the total cost. Let's say the bike costs $200. Next, decide how much to save each week. If you can save $5 each week, create a timeline. Your first milestone is $50, which you'll reach in 10 weeks. The next milestone is $100, achieved in 20 weeks. Continue this way until you reach your final goal of $200 in 40 weeks. Each milestone shows your progress and keeps you motivated.

| **Milestones** | **Weekly Savings** | | | | | | | | | |
|---|---|---|---|---|---|---|---|---|---|---|
| **1:** $50 | | | | | | | | | | |
| **2:** $100 | | | | | | | | | | |
| **3:** $200 | | | | | | | | | | |
| | | | | | | | | | | |

Another example is planning for a family trip. This can be a collaborative savings goal where everyone in the family contributes. Start by calculating the total cost of the trip. Include expenses like travel, accommodation, food, and activities. Let's say the trip costs $1,000. Next, determine how much each family member can save each month. If everyone can save $25 a month, that's $100 each month from the family. Create a timeline and set milestones. The first milestone could be $250, which will be reached in 2.5 months. The next milestone is $500, reached in 5 months. Continue until you reach the total amount needed for the trip.

Saving for big goals teaches you valuable lessons about planning, patience, and perseverance. It shows you that you can achieve anything with a clear plan and consistent effort. Whether saving for a bicycle, a family trip, or something else, remember to break down your goal into smaller steps, set milestones, and create a timeline. This makes the process manageable and keeps you motivated. Each small step brings you closer to your big dream.

## 3.6 EMERGENCY FUNDS: PREPARING FOR THE UNEXPECTED

Picture this: You're all set to buy that video game you've been saving for, and suddenly, your bike gets a flat tire. You need money for the repair but don't want to dip into your game savings. This is where an emergency fund comes in—it's your financial safety net for life's unexpected moments.

An emergency fund is a stash of money set aside for sudden expenses that pop up out of nowhere. Imagine your pet needing an emergency vet visit, your computer crashing before a big school project, or a surprise school trip requiring extra cash. These are the situations where having an emergency fund can save the day. It's *not* for buying new toys or treating yourself to a fun night out —it's there for real, urgent needs that can't wait.

### Building Your Emergency Fund

Starting an emergency fund might sound harsh, but it's easier than you think. Begin with a small goal, like $50 or $100. Setting a clear target helps you stay motivated. Once you reach that first goal, set a new one. Even small, regular contributions make a big difference. You can save a portion of your allowance or extra money you earn from chores. Consistency is critical—keep adding to it, even if it's just a few dollars at a time.

**When to Use It (and When Not To)**

Knowing when to dip into your emergency fund is as important as building it. Ask yourself: *Is this an urgent, necessary expense that can't wait?* If your dog needs surgery, that's an emergency. If you just want the latest comic book, it's not. Being smart about when to use your fund helps you preserve it for true emergencies. And once you've used part of your fund, focus on replenishing it—add a little extra each week until you're back to your target amount.

Let's do this activity to check off the emergencies:

- Your bike tire goes flat, and you must repair it to get to school.
- You want to buy the latest video game that just came out.
- Your pet gets sick and needs to visit the vet for urgent care.
- You want a new backpack because yours looks old, but it's still functional.
- Your favorite comic book released a new issue, and you want it now.
- Your computer breaks down the day before a school project is due, and you need it repaired quickly.
- You have an unexpected school field trip and need money for the bus and lunch.
- A family member's birthday party suddenly moves up, and you need a small gift.
- You've outgrown your shoes and need new ones for sports practice next week.
- Your favorite toy is on sale, and you feel like it's now or never.
- You lose your lunch money for the week and need to replace it.

- You want new clothes for the weekend, but your current wardrobe is fine.
- Your phone screen cracks, making it unusable, and you need it to stay in touch with family after school.
- Your friends will see a movie, and you want to join them.
- You want to buy new art supplies but still have some left at home.
- Your friend gets a new gaming console, and now you want one, too.

**Reflection Questions:**

Why is it essential to save emergency funds for true emergencies?

How did you decide if something was a real emergency or not?

What would happen if you spent your emergency fund on non-urgent things?

**Keep It Separate**

To avoid temptation, keep your emergency fund separate from your regular savings. If it's mixed in, you might accidentally (or purposely!) dip into it for non-emergencies. Whether you use a different jar or even a separate bank account, this clear separation will help you stay disciplined.

**Bonus: The Power of High-Yield Savings Accounts**

Let's add a bonus twist to your emergency fund: keeping it in a **High-Yield Savings Account** (HYSA). This type of account helps your money grow while it sits there, waiting for emergencies. Unlike a regular savings account, a HYSA earns more interest, meaning your emergency fund will quietly multiply over time. So, not only are you setting money aside for emergencies, but you're also making your money work for you!

### 3.7 FINDING THE RIGHT HYSA

Parents, when looking for the best High-Yield Savings Account, consider these key factors:

1. Interest Rate (APY): Look for the highest Annual Percentage Yield to maximize your savings. Some banks may offer promotional rates, so check that the rate remains competitive over time.
2. No Fees: Choose an account with no monthly fees or penalties for withdrawals. Every dollar counts when saving!
3. Minimum Balance: Ensure the account's minimum balance requirement is realistic so you don't get penalized.
4. FDIC Insurance: Ensure the account is FDIC-insured, so your money is safe, even if the bank faces financial trouble.
5. Access: Some accounts limit the number of withdrawals, usually six per month. Check if the account offers easy access to your funds when needed.
6. Customer Experience: Look for a bank that offers reliable customer service and easy-to-use tools, like a mobile app, to manage your savings.

By choosing a good HYSA, your emergency fund can grow while offering peace of mind. Even if you're not using the money, it's gaining interest and becoming an even bigger financial cushion.

Based on customer reviews and feedback reported by Top Consumers Review and Money.com, here are some of the best-rated high-yield savings accounts from the last few years:

1. Capital One—Known for its strong customer satisfaction, Capital One has consistently been praised for its competitive APY, no minimum deposit, and high ratings on customer service platforms like NerdWallet and Bankrate. It also offers a well-rated mobile app and no monthly fees, making it a top choice among major banks (Money)(Top Consumer Reviews).
2. Varo Bank – This online-only bank has received high marks for customer satisfaction, with an "A" rating from the Better Business Bureau (BBB). It offers a high APY and is well-regarded for its fee-free structure, automatic savings tools, and ease of use(Top Consumer Reviews).
3. Discover Bank – Discover's high-yield savings account stands out for its simple, user-friendly platform, high APY, and no minimum balance. Customers appreciate the lack of fees and the seamless digital experience(Money).
4. CIT Bank – Offering a competitive APY with a low minimum balance requirement, CIT Bank has garnered positive feedback for its ease of online account management and efficient mobile tools(Money).

Each of these banks has maintained a good reputation with customers and financial analysts, making them reliable choices for high-yield savings accounts.

Building and maintaining an emergency fund, whether in a jar or a high-yield account, gives you peace of mind. Without tapping into your other savings, you'll be ready for unexpected expenses—whether a vet visit, a bike repair, or something else. Plus, it teaches valuable financial habits that will benefit you for years to come. So, start small, stay consistent, and watch your safety net grow!

## 3.8 USING APPS TO TRACK SAVINGS: A BEGINNER'S GUIDE

Before the internet, we had to track our savings with a notebook and a pen. It got the job done, but let's be honest—it wasn't exactly exciting! Today, things are much easier and more exciting thanks to digital tools. Savings apps can help you manage your money with just a few taps on your phone. They offer easy access and real-time updates, so you always know how much you have saved. These apps make saving fun and interactive, turning what used to be a chore into something enjoyable.

Imagine having all your savings information right at your fingertips. With savings apps, you can see your balance grow in real-time. No more guessing how much you have or flipping through pages in a notebook. These apps let you input deposits, track progress, and even set savings goals. They make saving money feel like a game, with rewards and achievements. This keeps you engaged and motivated to save even more.

Let's discuss some kid-friendly savings apps that are perfect for young savers. RoosterMoney is a digital allowance and savings tracker app that helps kids understand how to budget and save. It offers features like goal-setting, tracking spending, and dividing money into categories like "spend," "save," and "give." It also allows parents to reward their kids for completing chores or achieving milestones. The app has fun visuals and is designed to be very user-friendly for kids.

Another fantastic app is Bankaroo. This is like a virtual bank for kids. It helps you keep track of your allowance, savings, and spending. The app is very user-friendly, making it easy for kids of all ages to use. You can set savings goals, track progress, and earn virtual badges for reaching milestones. Bankaroo also teaches you about important financial concepts like budgeting and saving for the future. It's a great way to learn about money management in a fun and interactive way.

Savings Spree is an educational game where kids learn about saving, spending, and investing. The app puts kids in charge of a character who earns money and faces real-life spending decisions. The goal is to teach kids how to save money and build healthy financial habits by making wise spending choices in the game.

Greenlight is a debit card and money management app designed for kids. It allows parents to control where kids can spend money, assign allowances, and track chores. Kids can set savings goals, learn about investing, and track spending habits. Greenlight emphasizes learning to save and budget while offering parental control.

There are many other apps designed to help kids learn the value of money, build good saving habits, and understand financial responsibility in an engaging and age-appropriate way. Parents can supervise their kids' progress while also helping them make smart financial decisions.

Setting up and using these apps is straightforward. You may start by creating an account. This usually involves choosing a username and password. Make sure to ask your parents for help if you need clarification. Once your account is set up, you can start inputting your deposits. Each time you save money, log it into the app. This keeps your savings record up-to-date. You can also set savings goals within the app. Decide what you want to save for and how much you need. The app will help you track your progress and keep you motivated.

Tracking your savings is simple with these apps. Each time you save money, enter the amount into the app. You can see your balance grow and watch as you get closer to your savings goals. The apps often have charts and graphs that show your progress visually. This makes it easier to understand how much you've saved and how far you still have to go. The real-time updates mean you always know exactly how much money you have.

Hearing about other kids' success with these apps can be very inspiring. One young saver, Mia, used a PiggyBot app to save for a new bicycle. She set up a savings pod in the app and tracked her progress every week. Seeing her savings grow motivated her, and she reached her goal in just a few months. Another kid, Alex, used Bankaroo to manage his allowance and save for a trip to the amusement park. He loved earning virtual badges and watching his savings increase. Mia and Alex found that using these apps made saving money fun and rewarding.

These success stories show how effective savings apps can be. They turn the sometimes tedious task of saving money into an engaging activity. With features like real-time updates, goal-setting, and interactive charts, these apps make it easier than ever to manage your savings. Whether saving for a big purchase, a particular trip, or just building your emergency fund, these apps can help you reach your goals.

Savings apps combine modern technology with financial education. They make saving easy, fun, and interactive, helping you build good money habits from a young age. With the right tools, you can take control of your finances and confidently work towards your goals. Why not give these apps a try? You might find that saving money is more fun than you ever imagined.

# 4

# SPENDING MONEY:

## MAKING INTELLIGENT SPENDING CHOICES AND UNDERSTANDING NEEDS VS. WANTS

For one of her birthdays, I decided to be that "cool" parent and gave my daughter money as a present. It was symbolic—ten bills of 10 at the age of 10, because who doesn't love a little math with their birthday cake? She could've bought anything her heart desired! But as the days went by, that money pulled a disappearing act. Curiosity got the best of me, so I asked her what she spent it on. Her response? A shrug, followed by the classic, "I dunno." It was like the money had evaporated into thin air. And that's when the lightbulb went on. Ah, yes—time to have the "smart money choices" talk!

## 4.1 SHOPPING SMART: COMPARING PRICES AND FINDING DEALS

First things first, let's talk about **comparing prices**. Imagine you want to buy a new game. You see it at one store for $50. But wait! Another store sells it for $40. That's a $10 difference! Comparing prices can save you a lot of money. It's like a treasure hunt, but you find savings instead of gold.

Online tools make price comparisons more effortless than ever. Websites like Google Shopping and PriceGrabber let you see prices from different stores all in one place. Just type in what you're looking for; these sites do the hard work for you. They show you the prices at various stores so you can choose the best deal. It's like having a super-smart shopping buddy who knows all the best prices.

In-store vs. online prices can be different, too. Sometimes, a store might have a higher price than its online counterpart. You can always check both. Buying online is cheaper, even after adding shipping costs. Some stores will even match their online prices if you show them. This way, you get the best deal without waiting for delivery. So, always compare prices both online and in-store before making a purchase.

**Finding deals** is another great way to save money. Couponing is a classic method. You may find coupons in newspapers, magazines, and online. Websites like Coupons.com offer printable coupons for all sorts of items. Also, BeFrugal, Rakuten, and Capital One Shopping. Clipping coupons might seem old-fashioned, but it's a great way to save money. You can even make it a fun activity with your family. Who can find the best coupon?

**Seasonal sales** are another goldmine for deals. Stores often have big sales during certain times of the year, like Black Friday, back-to-school, and holiday sales. Shopping during these times can save you a lot of money. Plan your purchases around these sales. If you want a new game, wait for a big sale. You'll get it at a much better price.

**Loyalty programs** are also worth looking into. Many stores offer memberships that give you access to special deals and rewards. These programs often have perks like discounts, points for every purchase, and even birthday bonuses. Join loyalty programs at stores you shop at frequently. You'll save money and get rewarded for your loyalty. It's a win-win!

Use the "Wait 24 Hours" Rule. If something catches your eye, you can practice waiting a day before buying it. This helps prevent impulse purchases and gives you time to think about whether you really want it.

Now, let's talk about **value over price**. Sometimes, the cheapest option isn't the best. Think about quality and how long something will last. For example, you might see a generic toy for $5 and a branded one for $10. The branded toy might be made of better materials and last longer. In the long run, you'll save money because you won't have to replace it as quickly.

Consider brand vs. generic items. Branded items often cost more, but they can be of higher quality. Generic items can be just as good, though. Compare the quality of both. Sometimes, the only difference is the name. Other times, the branded item is genuinely better. Make informed choices based on quality, not just price.

Let's also consider the item's lasting value: Is it worth it? *"Will I still use or like this a week from now or a year?"* This helps us decide whether something is worth buying.

Long-term savings come from investing in durable, high-quality items. Spending a bit more now can save you money in the future. For example, buying a sturdy backpack for school might cost more upfront, but it will last longer than a cheaper one. You won't have to buy a new one every year. Think about how long an item will last and whether it's worth spending a bit more.

Parents should lead by example. Demonstrate things like comparing prices, using coupons, or waiting for sales. Involve kids in Family Financial Decisions: show them how you decide between different purchases or why you choose specific products. This gives them a hands-on learning experience. Discuss Advertising Tricks: teach your kids how companies try to get them to spend money by making everything look "cool" or "necessary." Help them become critical consumers. Celebrate Smart Spending:

If your child makes a thoughtful decision to save, skip a purchase, or find a great deal, acknowledge and praise their choice. Positive reinforcement helps the lesson stick. Teach the Value of Delayed Gratification: Instill the idea that not everything needs to be bought immediately. Saving up for something larger or waiting for a sale can be more rewarding in the long run.

Let's practice some intelligent shopping with a fun exercise:

**Price Comparison Exercise**

1. Choose an item you want to buy, like a toy or game.
2. Use online tools like PriceGrabber or Google Shopping to compare prices at different stores.
3. Write down the prices you find.

4. Compare the prices and see which store offers the best deal.
5. Discuss the quality of the product and if it's a worthy purchase.

Next time you want to buy something, remember these tips: compare prices, look for deals, and consider value over price. These steps will help you make smart spending choices and save money. Happy shopping!

## 4.2 AVOIDING IMPULSE BUYS: PRACTICING PATIENCE

Impulse buying is when you buy something without planning. It's like seeing a candy bar at the checkout and grabbing it without thinking. This might seem harmless, but it can mess up your finances. Emotional spending is a big part of impulse buying. Maybe you feel excited, sad, or bored, and buying something makes you feel better. But these feelings don't last, and you end up with stuff you don't need. This kind of spending can derail your budget. You might spend money meant for important things, and suddenly, your financial plan is out of whack.

To avoid impulse buys, you need some strategies. One great tip is the 24-hour rule. If you see something you want, wait a day before buying it. This gives you time to think about whether you really need it. Often, the urge to buy will fade. Another helpful tip is to make a shopping list before you go to the store. Stick to this list, and you'll avoid buying extra items you didn't plan for. Setting spending limits is also intelligent. Allocate a fixed amount of money for discretionary spending each week. This helps you stay within your budget and think twice before making impulse buys.

**Mindful spending** means thinking carefully about each purchase. Start by asking yourself if you really need the item or just want it.

Needs are things you must have, like food and clothes. Wants are things you'd like to have but can live without, like toys or fancy gadgets. Reflect on your purchases to consider if they will bring long-term satisfaction. Will you still be happy with the item a week or a month from now? This practice helps you make thoughtful decisions and avoid buyer's remorse.

The feeling of regret after purchasing a product or service is known as "buyer's remorse:" it's the discomfort or disappointment a person experiences after purchasing, especially when they feel the item was unnecessary, too expensive, or underwhelming. This regret often stems from several factors. Impulse buying, for example, happens when a person makes a spontaneous purchase without much thought, only to realize later it wasn't worth the money. Another trigger is high expectations—when a product or service doesn't live up to what was anticipated, it can leave the buyer feeling let down. Additionally, financial guilt may arise if the purchase impacts one's budget or other priorities, making the person regret spending too much. There's also comparison dissatisfaction, where someone regrets their choice after finding a better deal elsewhere. Buyer's remorse is more common with larger purchases, like cars, electronics, or luxury items, but can happen even with smaller purchases. Making thoughtful, well-researched decisions can help reduce these feelings of regret and lead to more satisfying purchases.

Real-life scenarios can show the impact of impulse buying and the benefits of patience. Take the case of Sarah, who saw a shiny new toy at the store. She really wanted it but decided to wait and think about it. The next day, she realized she didn't need it and saved her money. Later, she used that money to buy a book she had been eyeing for months. She felt proud of her decision and enjoyed the book much more than she would have enjoyed the toy.

Another success story is about a boy named Jack. He wanted a new video game but knew it would blow his budget. He decided to wait and save up for it. During this time, he found a better game that was on sale. By being patient, he got a great deal and saved money. Jack learned that waiting can lead to better choices and more satisfaction.

Impulse buying might give you a quick thrill but can hurt your finances in the long run. Strategies like the 24-hour rule, making shopping lists, and setting spending limits can help you resist the urge. Mindful spending and reflecting on your purchases make thoughtful decisions easier. Real-life examples, like Sarah and Jack, show how patience can lead to smarter buys and greater satisfaction.

## 4.3 SPENDING ON EXPERIENCES VS. THINGS: WHAT MATTERS MORE?

Imagine you have some money saved up and are deciding between buying a new toy or going on a family trip. It's a tough choice, but let's consider each option's value. Spending on experiences can often be more fulfilling than buying things. Why? Because experiences create memories that last a lifetime. When you go on a trip or attend an event, you're not just buying a moment but building a memory you can cherish forever. These memories often bring more happiness than any toy could provide.

Experiences also help build social connections. When you do something fun with your family or friends, you create bonds that strengthen your relationships. Think about a family vacation where everyone laughs, explores new places, and shares meals. These moments bring you closer and create shared memories that you can talk about for years. Buying a toy might give you joy for a moment, but shared experiences leave a lasting impact.

Experiences will last much longer than any product or service purchased. A good experience or memory can bring back feelings of happiness and joy, even long after the moment has passed. Our brains are wired to store positive experiences deeply; recalling them is almost like reliving the event. The emotional power of a memory can trigger the same feelings of excitement, warmth, or contentment that we felt during the original moment simply by thinking about it. This is because our brains don't always distinguish between real-time experiences and vividly recalled memories.

There are many valuable experiences you can invest in. Family trips are a great example. Planning and saving for a vacation can be exciting. You can choose a destination, plan activities, and look forward to the adventure. One particularly rewarding type of trip is going on excursions and spending time in nature. Whether hiking through a national park, camping under the stars, or exploring forests and rivers, being in contact with nature can be rejuvenating and educational. It cultivates a deep connection to the environment, teaches respect for the natural world, and provides a peaceful escape from the busyness of daily life. Educational activities like workshops, classes, and camps are also outstanding. They allow you to learn new skills, meet new people, and explore new interests. Recreational activities like sports, hobbies, and entertainment can provide endless fun and growth. Joining a sports team, picking up a new hobby, or attending a concert can create beautiful memories and teach you new things.

Balancing spending on experiences and things is essential. It's okay to buy things you enjoy, but please keep in mind the value of experiences. Start by setting aside money for activities. Create a budget that includes funds for experiences you want to have. This way, you ensure you're not spending all your money on material items. Prioritize experiences that are meaningful and enriching. Choose activities that bring you joy and help you grow. This balance enables you to enjoy the best of both worlds.

Let's hear from some kids who found joy in spending on experiences. One child, Emma, had saved enough money to buy a new video game. But instead, she chose to use her savings for a family trip to the mountains. She loved every moment of the journey. She hiked, roasted marshmallows, and spent quality time with her family. The memories from that trip were far more valuable to her than the game she could have bought.

Another story is about a boy named Max. He had a choice between buying a new toy or signing up for a summer camp. He chose the camp and had the time of his life. He learned to build a robot, made new friends, and discovered a passion for science. The experience had a lasting impact on him, and he still talks about it years later. These stories show how experiences often bring more happiness and fulfillment than buying.

Spending on experiences can bring long-lasting joy and create beautiful memories. While having new toys and gadgets is nice, don't overlook the value of shared activities and adventures. Family trips, educational activities, and recreational experiences can enrich your life in ways material items cannot. Balancing your spending between things and experiences helps you enjoy the best of both worlds. So, next time you have some money to spend, consider investing in an experience that will bring you joy and create lasting memories.

## 4.4 UNDERSTANDING SALES AND DISCOUNTS: GETTING THE BEST VALUE

Sales and discounts can make shopping a lot more fun. They can also help you save money. However, understanding the different types of sales is critical. **Seasonal sales** are a big deal. Think about back-to-school sales, Black Friday, or holiday sales. These events happen every year and offer great deals on many items. Stores want to clear out their old stock, so they drop prices. **Clearance** sales are another type. These happen when stores intend to get rid of end-of-season items or discontinued products. You can find some real bargains during these sales. Remember, once these items are gone, they're not returning.

**Percentage discounts** are common, too. You might see signs like "20% off" or "Buy One, Get One 50% off." Understanding these discounts helps you see how much you're really saving. To calculate a percentage discount, multiply the original price by the discount rate. For example, if a $50 item is 20% off, multiply 50 by 0.20 to get 10: that's the amount discounted. Subtract that ten from 50, and the item now costs $40. Simple, right? This math helps you see if a deal is worth it.

Spotting genuine sales is essential. Some sales are **just marketing tricks**. Always compare the original price with the sale price. Check prices before and during sales to see if you're getting a real deal. Some stores raise the original price just before a sale to make the discount look bigger. Reading the fine print also helps. Some sales have terms and conditions that limit the discount. The sale may only be on specific items or brands. Knowing these details enables you to avoid surprises at the checkout.

Planning ahead for sales can save you time and money. Make a list of items you want to buy during sales events. This helps you stay focused and keep away impulse buys. Stick to your budget, even when you see terrific deals. It's easy to get carried away during sales, but remember, you're trying to save money. Combining discounts can also maximize your savings. Use coupons and loyalty points with sale prices for even better deals. Stores often allow you to stack these savings, so take full advantage.

Let's look at a success story. Jenny wanted a new tablet. She knew Black Friday was coming up and started checking prices a few weeks before. Jenny found the tablet she wanted for $300. The price dropped to $200 on Black Friday, and this girl had a $20 coupon from her loyalty program. She ended up paying $180 for a tablet that was originally $300. Jenny's patience and planning paid off big time.

Here's a **practical exercise** to help you understand sales better:

Calculating the Final Price After a Discount

1. Find an item you like with a percentage discount.
2. Write down the original price and the discount rate.
3. Multiply the original price by the discount rate to obtain the discount amount.
4. Subtract the discount amount from the original price to get the final price.
5. Compare this with the original price to see how much you saved.

Funny tip: a friend of mine doing this exercise, found his Personal Computer, and he grabbed it!

Understanding sales and discounts helps you get the best value for your money. By knowing the types of sales, spotting real deals, and combining discounts, you can shop smart and save big.

## 4.5 THE TRUE COST OF OWNERSHIP: BEYOND THE PRICE TAG

The price tag isn't the only cost you must consider when you buy something. The actual cost of ownership includes maintenance, operating costs, and depreciation. **Maintenance costs** are what you spend to keep an item in good condition. For example, if you buy a bike, you must pay for tire repairs and tune-ups. These costs can add up over time. **Operating costs** are what you spend to use the item. For a bike, this might include buying a helmet and bike lock. For a computer, it includes electricity and internet service. **Depreciation** is the loss of value over time. Most items lose value as they get older and worn out.

To calculate the actual cost of owning something, start with the initial price. Add any expected maintenance and operating costs. Then, think about how long you'll use the item and how much it will be worth when you're done with it. This gives you a better idea of the total cost. Comparing alternatives helps, too. You could choose between two bikes. One costs more upfront but has lower maintenance costs. The other is cheaper but needs frequent repairs. Weighing these factors helps you make an intelligent choice.

Thoughtful purchasing decisions save you money in the long run. Choose items that offer good value over time. Spending more on a high-quality item can be cheaper in the end. You won't have to replace it as often. Also, be aware of hidden costs. Some items have extra expenses that aren't obvious at first. For example, a cheap printer might have expensive ink cartridges. Knowing these hidden costs helps you avoid surprises.

Let's look at an example. Owning a pet is a big responsibility. The price of the pet is just the beginning. You'll need to buy food, toys, and bedding. Vet visits and grooming add to the cost. Over time, these expenses add up. Before getting a pet, calculate these costs to see if you can afford it.

Another example is comparing the cost of different bikes. One might be cheaper but need more repairs. The other might cost more upfront but last longer with less maintenance. Comparing the total cost helps you choose the better deal.

Understanding the actual cost of ownership helps you make more intelligent choices. By considering maintenance, operating costs, and depreciation, you see the actual price of an item. This way, you can choose items that offer the best value and avoid hidden expenses.

**Interactive Activity**

Parents, let's play this: "The True Cost of Ownership Challenge."

**Step 1: Introduction**

Start by explaining to participants that an item's price tag isn't the only cost they need to consider. Mention the three main hidden costs: maintenance, operating costs, and depreciation.

**Step 2: Item Selection**

Present the group with a list of everyday items, such as:

- Bike
- Smartphone
- Computer
- Car
- Video game console
- Pet (dog or cat)

**Step 3: Cost Breakdown**

For each item, guide the participants through the three types of costs. For example:

- Bike:
- Maintenance costs: Tire repairs, tune-ups
- Operating costs: Helmet, bike lock
- Depreciation: Over time, the bike will lose value

Use other items from the list and invite participants to develop their own examples of hidden costs. This helps reinforce the concept.

**Step 4: The True Cost Worksheet**

Provide each participant with a worksheet where they can fill in the following details for a selected item:

- Purchase Price (from the price tag)
- Maintenance Costs (per year)
- Operating Costs (per year)
- Depreciation (how much the item's value decreases each year)

Example for a bike:

- Purchase price: $200
- Maintenance costs: $50 per year (tire repairs, tune-ups)
- Operating costs: $30 (helmet and bike lock)
- Depreciation: $40 per year (estimated loss in value)

**Step 5: True Cost Calculation**

Guide participants in adding up the total cost of ownership over a set period (e.g., five years). The formula is:

- Total cost = Purchase price + (Maintenance costs x years) + (Operating costs x years) + Depreciation x years)

Example for a bike over five years:

- Total cost = $200 + ($50 x 5) + ($30 x 5) + ($40 x 5) = $700

**Step 6: Reflection and Discussion**

- "Was the final cost more than you expected?"
- "What could you do to lower the total cost of ownership?"
- "Are there any purchases you would reconsider based on the true cost?"

**Step 7: Bonus Challenge:**

- Offer a fun challenge where participants find an item in their home, calculate its true cost, and share their findings with the group. This makes the activity more interactive and helps reinforce the concept.

- Outcome: By the end of the activity, participants will have a clearer understanding of the actual cost of ownership. They'll be more aware of the long-term expenses tied to their purchases and better equipped to make wise spending choices!

## 4.6 USING PREPAID CARDS: SAFE SPENDING FOR KIDS

Prepaid cards are a great way to manage money. They work like gift cards but can be reloaded with funds. Unlike credit cards, you can only spend what's on the card. This helps you control your spending. There are different types of prepaid cards. Gift cards are for specific stores or restaurants. Reloadable prepaid cards can be used anywhere that accepts debit cards. They're like mini bank accounts you can carry in your pocket.

Using prepaid cards has many benefits. They limit your spending to the amount on the card, so you can't overspend. This makes them a safe option for kids. You don't have to carry cash, reducing the risk of losing money. Prepaid cards also teach budgeting and spending habits. You learn to manage your money and make it last. It's excellent practice for using a regular bank account in the future.

To use a prepaid card, you first need to activate it. Follow the instructions that come with the card. This might involve calling a number or visiting a website. Once activated, you can start using the card. Keep track of your balance to make sure you have enough funds. Most cards let you check your balance online or through an app. Reloading the card is easy. You can add money at a store, online, or through a bank transfer.

Here's an example. Mia uses a prepaid card for her school lunches. Her parents load the card with money each month. Mia tracks her spending and knows how much she has left. This helps her budget for the week. She's learned to manage her money and avoid overspending. Keeping a spending log is a practical tip. Write down each purchase to see where your money goes. This helps you stay on budget and make better spending choices.

# MAKE A DIFFERENCE WITH YOUR REVIEW

## UNLOCK THE POWER OF TEACHING

**"Money isn't everything, but teaching it can change everything."**

— ANONYMOUS

When you help others, you're not just giving; you're shaping futures. Let's work together to build brighter ones!

Would you like to help a parent or kid who's eager to learn about money but doesn't know where to start? I wrote *Money Skills for Kids and Parents* to make understanding money simple, fun, and something the whole family can enjoy.

But to reach more families like yours, I need your help!

Most people choose books based on reviews, and your words could guide another parent or teacher on this exciting journey. Imagine your review helping just one more family to:

- Teach their kids how to save for their first big purchase.
- Show a young entrepreneur how to turn a hobby into a business.
- Inspire smart spending habits for a lifetime of financial freedom.

Leaving a review takes less than a minute but can make a huge impact on someone's money skills journey. It's free, quick, and could be the spark that changes another family's financial future!

To leave a review, just scan the QR code below or visit: https://www.amazon.com/review/create-review?asin=B0DM2NW2Z8

If you love helping others grow, you're exactly the person we hoped to reach with this book. Thank you from the bottom of our heart!

**Kingtheros Publishing**

# 5

# INVESTING MONEY:

## AN INTRODUCTION TO INVESTING AND HOW IT CAN GROW YOUR MONEY OVER TIME

As a kid, I found a dusty roll of old money in a drawer. There were also a few coins and a note from my grandpa saying, "Plant these seeds wisely." I thought he meant actual seeds, so I tried to grow that money tree. I had seen my beans growing in a school experiment, so this might also work. Spoiler alert: It didn't. But it sparked my curiosity about raising money.

### 5.1 WHAT IS INVESTING? SIMPLE EXPLANATIONS

Investing is like planting a seed that grows into a tree. You put your money into something; over time, it can develop into more money. Think of it as giving your money a job to do. Instead of sitting in your piggy bank, your money gets to work and earns more. It's like magic, but real!

I like to think of investing as planting the seeds of a single corncob. When it's planted in the right conditions and well cared for, it has the potential to grow into dozens of plants, each yielding even more.

People invest for several reasons. One big reason is to build wealth. Imagine you want to buy a car one day. Saving money is great, but investing can help your money grow faster. This means you can reach your goals sooner. Investing also helps with financial security. It gives you a safety net for the future. If you invest wisely, you can have money for emergencies or significant life events like going to college or buying a house. It's like having a financial superpower.

Now, let's talk about the **difference between saving and investing**. Saving money in a bank is like keeping it safe in a vault. It's there when you need it, and it earns a little bit of interest. But it's slow and steady. Investing, on the other hand, can bring more significant rewards. But it also comes with risks. When you invest, there's a chance you could lose some or all of your money. This is called risk. The possibility of making money is called a return. The greater the risk, the greater the potential reward. But remember, with higher risk comes the chance of losing more.

Another key difference is the **time horizon**. Saving is usually for short-term goals. You might save for a new bike or a holiday trip. Investing is for long-term goals. It's like planning for the future, such as going to college or buying a house. When you invest, you're thinking about what you want in the next few years or even decades. This long-term view helps you ride out the ups and downs of the market.

Let's introduce some basic investment concepts. First up is a **risk**. This is the chance that your investment might lose value. Think of it like riding a rollercoaster. There are highs and lows, and it's not always predictable. Next is **return**. This is the money you make from your investment. It's like the fruits that grow on your money tree. The goal is to have more fruits over time. Finally, there's **diversification**. This means spreading your investments on different types of assets. It's like planting various kinds of seeds in your garden. If one plant doesn't do well, others might still thrive.

Investing can feel like a rollercoaster, but it's a ride worth taking. It helps you grow your money and reach your financial goals. Just remember to start small, understand the risks, and think long-term. And remember to diversify your investments. Having a mix of different investments can reduce risk and increase your chances of success.

So, think of investing as planting seeds for your future. With patience, care, and some knowledge, those seeds can grow into a solid financial tree. Start learning, start planting, and watch your money grow!

## 5.2 UNDERSTANDING STOCKS: OWNING PART OF A COMPANY

Imagine you're at a birthday party with a giant cake. Everyone wants a piece. Stocks are like slices of that cake, but instead of cake, you're getting a piece of a company. When you buy a stock, you own a small part of that company. It's like having a tiny slice of the company pie. This means you get to share in the company's ups and downs. If the company does well, your slice becomes more valuable. If it doesn't, your slice might shrink.

So, how do stocks work? Stocks are bought and sold in a place called the **stock market**. Think of it like a farmer's market, but instead of fruits and veggies, you're trading pieces of companies. The price of a stock is called its share price. This price can go up or down depending on how well the company is doing and how much people want to buy or sell its stocks. If many people want to buy the stock, the price increases. If lots of people want to sell, the price goes down.

Some companies also pay dividends to their shareholders. **Dividends** are like little thank-you notes with money. When a company makes a profit, it might share some of that money with its shareholders. These are called dividends. For example, if you own stock in a company that pays dividends, you might get a small payment every few months. It's like getting a bonus just for owning the stock. Not all companies pay dividends, but those that do often attract investors looking for steady income.

Let's look at some popular stocks that you might recognize. Companies like Apple, Disney, and Nike are well-known brands. If you own a stock in Apple, you own a tiny part of the company that makes iPhones and iPads. If you own a stock in Disney, you own a slice of the magic kingdom that creates movies and runs theme parks. If you own a stock in Nike, you have a share in the company that makes those cool sneakers. Over time, investing in these companies has been profitable for many people. For example, if you had invested in Apple years ago, your investment would have grown significantly as the company introduced new products and expanded its market.

Buying and selling stocks can lead to profits or losses. If you buy a stock at a low price and sell it at a high price, you make a profit. But if you buy it at a high price and sell it at a lower price, you lose money. This is why it's essential to understand what you're investing in and to have a plan. The stock market can be unpredictable, but you can make informed choices with knowledge and patience.

One real-life example of investing in popular companies is the story of a boy named Alex. Alex loved playing video games and decided to invest in a company that makes them. He bought a few shares of the company with his allowance. Over the years, the company released popular games, and the stock price increased. Alex's small investment grew, and he learned a valuable lesson about the power of investing in things he understood and believed in.

Investing in stocks is like owning a piece of a company pie. When you buy stocks, you become a part-owner of that company. The stock market is where these pieces are traded, and the share price tells you how much a stock is worth. Dividends are extra rewards that some companies give to their shareholders. Popular companies like Apple, Disney, and Nike have been suitable investments for many people. Buying and selling stocks can lead to profits or losses, so knowing what you're doing is essential. With some knowledge and patience, you can make informed choices and watch your investments grow.

## 5.3 EXCHANGE-TRADED FUNDS: LOTS OF COMPANIES AT ONCE

Exchange-traded funds, or **ETFs**, are like baskets in a market. Imagine one basket filled with fruits, another with eggs, and a third with candies. Each basket holds different things, but all within the same category. ETFs work similarly, except they hold groups of companies instead of fruits or eggs. For example, one ETF might have stocks from technology companies, while another might have stocks from food or medicine companies. Investing in an ETF is like buying the whole basket—your money is spread across many companies simultaneously. This helps reduce risk because you're not just relying on one company to do well.

Here are three popular and important ETFs in the stock market and some of the big companies they hold. These ETFs have funny names, but once you start learning more about investing, they'll make sense:

1. SPDR S&P 500 ETF Trust (SPY): This ETF tracks the performance of the 500 largest companies in the U.S., including Apple, Microsoft, and Amazon.
2. Invesco QQQ Trust (QQQ): This ETF follows 100 of the biggest non-financial companies listed on the Nasdaq stock market, such as Nvidia and Meta.
3. iShares MSCI Emerging Markets ETF (EEM): This ETF focuses on companies from developing countries, including Samsung Electronics, Alibaba Group, and Taiwan Semiconductor Manufacturing.

By investing in ETFs, you spread your money across many companies simultaneously, making it safer while aiming for growth.

## 5.4 ASSETS: THINGS THAT PAY YOU MONEY REGULARLY

While some people invest in stocks, others prefer to invest in assets that generate money (cash flow)—these are things that pay you money regularly, like rental properties, businesses, or even certain types of investments like dividend-paying stocks. The exciting thing about cash flow investments is that they don't just sit there hoping to grow in value. They put money in your pocket

over time, whether rent from a property, profits from a business, or interest from a loan you've made.

The real magic happens when you take that cash flow and reinvest it. Instead of just spending the money, you can use it to buy more assets that also produce cash flow. Let's say you open a lemonade stand, and it does so well that you earn enough money to open a second stand in a different neighborhood. Your cousin will run the new stand and earn a percentage of the profits for their work. Again, it's like planting one seed, and as the plant grows and bears fruit, you collect those seeds and plant even more. Over time, you have a whole garden of assets, all working to grow your wealth. This process of reinvesting cash flow into more assets creates a compounding effect, where your investments grow faster and faster, giving you more opportunities to continue expanding your financial garden.

By investing in cashflowing assets and reinvesting the profits, you're building a system that works for you, even while you sleep. It's one of the most powerful ways to grow wealth over time!

## 5.5 BONDS AND SAVINGS ACCOUNTS: SAFE INVESTMENT OPTIONS

Imagine you lend your friend $10, and they promise to pay you back $11 next week. That extra dollar is like the interest you earn on a bond. Bonds work similarly but involve lending money to companies or governments. When you buy a bond, you're giving a loan. In return, they pay you interest over time. Eventually, they repay the original amount you lent. It's like being a mini-banker!

There are different types of bonds. Government bonds are loans to the government. These are considered very safe because the government backs them. Corporate bonds are loans to companies. These can be riskier than government bonds but often pay more interest. So, if you lend money to a big company like Apple, it's a corporate bond. The company uses the money to grow its business and pays you back with interest.

As we have seen before, savings accounts are another safe way to grow your money. Unlike bonds, savings accounts are low-risk. You deposit your money in a bank, and the bank pays you interest. This interest adds up over time, making your money grow. Savings accounts are also very accessible. You can take out your money whenever you need it. This makes them an excellent option for short-term goals or emergency funds. You earn a little interest, and your money is safe and easy to access.

How do bonds and savings accounts compare? First, let's talk about risk. Savings accounts have shallow risk. Your money is safe in the bank, and you earn a small interest. Bonds have varied risk levels. Government bonds are safer, while corporate bonds can be riskier but offer higher returns. Next, consider liquidity, which is how easily you can access your money. Savings accounts are highly liquid. You can withdraw your money anytime. Bonds are less liquid. You might have to wait until the bond matures to get your money back. Lastly, let's look at return rates. Savings accounts typically offer lower returns. They are safe, but the interest you earn is small. Bonds usually offer higher returns, especially corporate bonds, but they are more risky.

Imagine you have $100. If you put it in a savings account with a 1% interest rate, you'll earn $1 a year. It's safe and easy, but the return is small. If you buy a government bond with a 3% interest rate, you'll earn $3 a year. It's still safe, but you must wait to get your money back. Buying a corporate bond with a 5% interest rate will earn $5 in a year. The return is higher, but there's a bit more risk involved.

So, whether you choose a savings account or bonds depends on your goals and how comfortable you are with risk. If you want safety and easy access to your money, a savings account is a good choice. If you're okay with a bit more risk for higher returns and don't need the money immediately, bonds might be the way to go. Both options can help you grow your money over time, each with its own benefits.

One real-life example is a family saving for a vacation. They put some money in a savings account for easy access and safety. They also buy a few government bonds to earn a bit more interest. Over time, their savings grow, and they have enough money for a fun trip. Another example is a young investor named Sam. He uses his allowance to buy corporate bonds from a well-known company. The bonds pay good interest, and he saved a nice sum of money after a few years.

The most common way to buy bonds is through an online brokerage account or a financial advisor. Some popular brokerage firms that offer access to both corporate and government bonds include Fidelity, Vanguard, and Charles Schwab. You can buy U.S. government bonds directly from the government through TreasuryDirect.gov. Treasury bonds, bills, and notes are available there without a broker. This is the official website of the U.S. Department of the Treasury.

Bonds and savings accounts are like financial tools in your toolbox. Each has its strengths and uses. Knowing how they work helps you wisely choose where to put your money. Understanding these options is vital whether you're saving for something special or just want to grow your money safely. So, consider your goals, risk comfort, and choose the best option. Your financial future will thank you.

## 5.6 THE ROLE OF INTEREST: HOW YOUR MONEY GROWS

Imagine you have a magical tree that grows money instead of apples. This tree doesn't just give you one coin for every coin you plant. Instead, it gives you more coins over time. That's what interest does for your money. Interest is the extra money you earn from your initial investment. You earn interest when you put your money into a savings account or a bond. This can be simple or compound interest.

**Simple interest** is the most straightforward. It's calculated only based on the initial amount of money you put in, which is called the principal. For example, if you invest $100 at a simple interest rate of 5% annually, you earn $5 annually. After one year, you have $105. After two years, you have $110, and so on. It's a steady way to grow your money but not as exciting as compound interest.

**Compound interest** is where the magic happens. It's calculated on both the initial principal and the interest that has already been added. This means you earn interest on your interest. Imagine you invest $100 at a compound interest rate of 5% per year. After one year, you earn $5, totaling $105. In the second year, you earn interest on $105, not just the original $100. So, you earn $5.25, making your total $110.25. This snowball effect means your money grows faster over time.

The power of compound interest is truly unique. It's like a snowball rolling down a hill, gaining more snow, and getting bigger. A small initial investment can grow exponentially. For example, if you invest $100 at a compound interest rate of 5% per year, it

grows to $105 after one year, $110.25 after two years, and keeps growing. The longer you leave it, the more it grows. Over 20 years, that $100 can turn into $265. This shows how powerful compound interest can be over time.

Different interest rates can significantly impact how much your investment grows. Let's compare a 1% interest rate with a 5% interest rate. If you invest $100 at 1% simple interest, you earn $1 each year. After ten years, you have $110. If you invest $100 at 5% simple interest, you earn $5 each year. After ten years, you have $150. The difference is even more dramatic with compound interest. At 1%, your $100 grows to about $110.46 in ten years. At 5%, it grows to about $162.89. Higher interest rates mean faster growth.

To see this in action, try some interactive calculations. Grab a sheet of paper or use an online interest calculator. Start with a simple interest calculation. After five years, how much will you have if you invest $100 at 3% simple interest? (Answer: $115). Now, try a compound interest calculation. If you invest $100 at 3% compound interest, how much will you have after five years? (Answer: about $115.93). These exercises show how different interest rates and types of interest can affect your investment.

Interest is like a magical tree that helps your money grow. Simple interest adds a steady amount each year, while compound interest accelerates growth by adding interest to your interest. The power of compound interest can turn small investments into significant sums over time. Different interest rates can significantly affect how much your money grows. By understanding how interest works, you can make intelligent choices about where to put your money and watch it grow.

## 5.7 INVESTING GAMES: LEARNING THROUGH SIMULATION

Imagine learning about investing by playing games. Sounds fun, right? Investing games are a great way to understand how the stock market works without risking real money. These games make learning about money interactive and enjoyable. You can play stock market simulators, which are virtual platforms for trading stocks. You get to practice buying and selling stocks as in the real market. It's like a test run before you start using real money. Another option is investment board games. These teach you strategies and concepts in a playful setting. They are perfect for family game nights.

Several popular investing games can help you get started. Monopoly is a classic board game that teaches you about property investment and money management. You buy properties, collect rent, and try to bankrupt your opponents. It's a fun way to learn about managing assets and making strategic decisions. Cashflow Classic by Robert Kiyosaki teaches the basics of personal finance, cash flow management, and investing in assets like stocks, real estate, and businesses. Investopedia Stock Simulator helps you practice trading with virtual money and shows how the stock market works and how to use an online brokerage. Another great game is The Stock Market Game. This game simulates real stock trading. You get a virtual portfolio and make investment decisions based on actual market data. It's a safe way to practice investing without any financial risk.

These games are more than just fun. They also have educational benefits. They help you understand investment concepts by applying them in real-world scenarios. For example, when you play Monopoly, you learn about buying properties, managing cash flow, and making investment decisions. These are real-world skills that can help you in the future. Investing games also teach you decision-making skills. You learn to make informed choices based on available information. This is crucial in the real world, where making sound investment decisions can lead to financial success.

Setting up accounts for online simulators is easy. First, choose a simulator that you like. Many are free and easy to use. Register with your email and create a password. Once your account is set up, you can start practicing. The game rules are usually straightforward. Read through the instructions to understand how to play. Each game has different objectives, so know what you're aiming for. Focus on the educational outcomes. These games are designed to teach you about investing, so pay attention to what you learn. Take notes on strategies that work and those that don't. This way, you can apply these lessons when investing with real money.

Playing investing games with your family can be a great bonding activity. You can all learn together and discuss strategies. It makes learning about investing a shared experience. You can set up mini-competitions to see who can grow their virtual portfolio the most. This adds a fun element and keeps everyone engaged. Plus, discussing your decisions and strategies helps reinforce what you've learned. You see different perspectives and learn from each other's mistakes and successes.

One practical tip is to start small. Don't try to make big moves right away. Focus on understanding the basics. As you get more comfortable, you can try more advanced strategies. Another tip is to be patient. Like real investing, these games require patience. Don't get discouraged if you don't see immediate results. The goal is to learn and improve over time. Lastly, have fun! These games are designed to make learning about investing enjoyable. The more fun you have, the more you'll want to keep playing and learning.

Investing games offer a unique way to learn about money. They combine fun and education, making complex concepts easier to understand. Whether you're practicing with stock market simulators or playing board games like Monopoly, these games provide valuable lessons. They teach you about making informed decisions, managing assets, and understanding market trends. So grab a game, gather your family, and start learning about investing in a fun and interactive way.

## 5.8 STARTING WITH SMALL INVESTMENTS: EASY STEPS FOR BEGINNERS

When I first thought about investing, it felt like climbing a mountain without a map. But I soon learned that starting small can make a huge difference. Beginning with tiny investments helps build confidence and experience. You don't need a lot of money to get started. Micro-investing apps like Acorns and Stash are fantastic for beginners. They allow you to invest small amounts, even spare change from everyday purchases. For example, if you buy a coffee for $2.75, these apps round it up to $3 and invest the extra $0.25. It's an easy way to dip your toes into investing without feeling overwhelmed.

Another great way to start small is by buying fractional shares. This means you can purchase portions of expensive stocks. Imagine investing in a big company like Amazon but needing more money to buy a total share. Fractional shares let you buy just a part of that share. This makes it affordable to invest in well-known companies even with a limited budget. Apps like SoFi Invest offer commission-free trading on stocks and ETFs, plus cryptocurrency investing. Provides access to educational resources, making it ideal for beginners. Betterment and Wealthfront are robo-advisors that automatically invest your money in a diversified portfolio of ETFs.

Let's walk through how you and your parents can make your first investments together. It's simple and fun!

**Step 1: Pick a Platform**

First, choose an app or website to invest with. The ones we shared earlier are easy to use, especially for beginners. To get started, create an account and connect it to your bank. You must enter basic info, like your name and email, and create a strong password.

**Step 2: Choose What to Invest In**

Now, it's time to pick your investments! This is where you and your parents can do some research together. Consider what you're interested in—technology, sports, or entertainment. You can look at companies, ETFs (which are like baskets of stocks), or even bonds. Check how well they're doing. If you love tech, you might want to explore big companies like Apple or Google. Understanding what you're investing in is essential, so read up, watch videos, and ask your parents for help.

**Step 3: Make Your First Investment**

After you've chosen, decide how much you want to invest. You don't need much money—starting with $5 or $10 is perfectly fine. Use the app to buy your stock or bond. Congrats! You've just made your first investment! Now, you can watch it grow over time.

**Step 4: Do Your Homework**

When investing, research is vital. Start by looking at how well the company is doing. Are they making money? Do people like their products? Understanding these things will help you make intelligent decisions. Also, keep an eye on market trends. If a particular industry, like technology, is doing well, it might be a good time to invest in tech companies. Staying informed by reading the news or asking questions will help you make even better choices in the future!

Now, you're ready to start investing!

Hearing success stories can be inspiring. Take the story of a young girl named Emma. She started investing with just $50 using a micro-investing app. She chose to invest in eco-friendly companies because she cared about the environment. Over a few years, her small investments grew, and she learned valuable lessons about patience and research. Daniil started investing at just 12 years old after reading books on personal finance and getting guidance from his father. He began with a small amount of money, buying shares of companies he knew and understood, such as Apple and Microsoft. When he reached his late teens, Daniil regularly spoke at financial conferences and encouraged other young people to start investing early. Jaden Carr, a 10-year-old from Texas, received a gift of 10 shares of GameStop stock from his mom in 2019 as a way to teach him about investing. When GameStop stock skyrocketed during the 2021 "short squeeze," Jaden sold his shares for over $3,000!

Another example is David, a teenager who bought fractional shares in a popular tech company. He started with birthday money and watched his investment grow as the company released new products. All these kids started small, but their investments taught them important financial lessons.

Starting with small investments is like taking baby steps. It helps build your confidence and teaches you the basics of investing. Using micro-investing apps and buying fractional shares makes it accessible and easy. Research is your first best friend—it helps you make informed choices and avoid mistakes. The second one is time—the earlier you start, the better. Remember, every prominent investor started small. Your small investments can grow into something big with patience and smart choices. Keep learning, keep investing, and watch your money grow!

# 6

# DIGITAL FINANCIAL TOOLS:

## NAVIGATING THE MODERN WORLD

Have you ever wished you could pay for something by just waving your phone? Imagine this: you're at the ice cream shop, and instead of digging through your pockets for coins, you simply tap your phone, and voilà! You've paid. Welcome to the world of digital wallets and apps. They make managing money as easy as pie, and yes, that means more time to enjoy your ice cream.

### 6.1 DIGITAL WALLETS AND APPS: MANAGING MONEY ONLINE

Digital wallets are like a magic trick for your money. Instead of carrying cash or cards, you store your payment information on your phone. This makes it super easy to pay for things. Digital wallets are apps that hold your debit or credit card info, so you don't need to carry physical cards. Think of them as a virtual wallet that lives on your phone. Popular examples include Apple Pay, Google Wallet, Google Pay, PayPal and Samsung Pay. These apps securely store your payment details and let you pay with just a tap.

There are many benefits to using digital wallets. First, they make transactions quick and contactless. Imagine you're in a hurry at the grocery store. Instead of fumbling with cash or cards, you just tap your phone, and the payment is done. This is super convenient and saves time. Digital wallets also come with top-notch security features. They use encryption, which scrambles your info to keep it safe. Some even use biometric authentication, like fingerprints or face recognition. This means only you can access your wallet. So, even if you lose your phone, your money stays safe.

Setting up a digital wallet is a breeze. First, download the app you want to use. Open the app and follow the instructions to add your card information. This usually involves **taking a** picture of your card or entering the details manually. Next, link your bank account if needed. The app will guide you through this process. Once your card is added, you're ready to make payments. At the store, look for the contactless payment symbol. Open your digital wallet, tap your phone near the payment terminal, and await confirmation. That's it! You've just made a payment without touching your wallet.

Digital wallets aren't just for adults. There are kid-friendly financial apps that help manage money digitally, as before-mentioned there are Greenlight, Bankaroo, RoosterMoney, and others.

Imagine you're saving for a new bike. You can use Bankaroo to set a savings goal and track your progress. Each time you get your allowance, you log it in the app. You can see how close you are to reaching your goal. You can set up different accounts, like one for saving, another for spending, and a third one for sharing. This helps you manage your money better and decide how much to save and how much to spend. These apps make learning about money fun and interactive.

Digital wallets and financial apps are changing the way we handle money. They make transactions quick, secure, and convenient. Using these tools allows you to manage your money better and learn valuable financial skills. So, next time you're at the ice cream shop, just tap your phone and enjoy your treat. Your phone's got your back.

## 6.2 INTRODUCTION TO ONLINE BANKING: SAFETY AND SECURITY

Online banking is like having a bank branch right in your living room. Instead of going to the bank in person, you can manage your accounts online from your computer or smartphone. This digital access makes it easy to check your balance, transfer money, pay bills, and even monitor your transactions. Think of it as your personal bank manager who works 24/7, never takes a vacation, and is always ready to help you manage your money.

The benefits of online banking are huge. Imagine needing to transfer money to a friend at midnight. You can do online banking instantly without waiting for the bank to open. You have access to your accounts anytime, anywhere. Another great thing is paperless statements. You can view your bank statements online, which reduces clutter and helps the environment. No more piles of paper on your desk! This also means you can find any transaction easily without digging through old papers.

Setting up an online banking account is simple. First, visit your bank's website and look for the online banking section. You'll need to create an account by entering your details, like your name, address, and account number. The bank might send you a verification code to your phone or email. Once you verify, you can create a username and a strong password. Now you're ready to log in. When you log in, you'll see a dashboard. This is where you can view your accounts, check your balance, and see recent transactions. It may look confusing at first but don't worry. Take your time to explore the different sections. Most banks have tutorials to help you understand the interface.

**Tip**: some banks give bonuses for opening an account with them, and parents may help you find the offer. It's always a good idea to get free money!

Performing transactions online is easy. Want to transfer money to a friend? Go to the transfers section, enter your friend's account details and the amount you want to send. Click "transfer," and it's done. Most banks have a Zelle app where you just need to put your friend's phone number to transfer if they also have Zelle. Need to pay a bill? Go to the bill pay section and enter the biller's details and the amount. Click "pay," and you're set. You can also set up automatic payments for regular bills, like your phone or internet, so you never miss a payment.

Keeping your online banking information secure is super important. Start with a strong password. Use a mix of letters, numbers, and special characters. Avoid using evident things like your name or birthday. Change your password regularly. It's always a good idea to have a notebook in a safe place where we store all our passwords if you don't want to share them with Google. Every day in our lives, we're entering new websites and apps that require passwords, and having the same password for every place is not very "healthy." Two-factor authentication adds an extra layer of security. This means you'll need to enter a code sent to your phone or email in addition to your password. It's like having a double lock on your door. Even if someone guesses your password, they won't get in without the code.

**Safe Banking Checklist**

- Create a strong password: Use a mix of letters, numbers, and special characters.
- Enable two-factor authentication: Adds an extra layer of security.
- Update your software: Keep your banking apps and devices updated to protect against new threats.
- Avoid public Wi-Fi: Use secure networks to access your accounts.
- Monitor your accounts: Regularly check your transactions for any suspicious activity.

Online banking brings convenience and security to managing your money. Features like 24/7 access and paperless statements make banking more accessible and eco-friendly. Setting up your account is a breeze, and performing transactions is straightforward. Just remember to keep your information secure with strong passwords and two-factor authentication.

## 6.3 USING BUDGETING APPS: TOOLS TO STAY ON TRACK

Have you ever wondered where all your allowance money went by the end of the week? You know you had some cash, but now it's all gone, and you can't remember what you spent it on. That's where budgeting apps come in handy. These digital tools help you keep track of your income and expenses. They are like a personal finance assistant right in your pocket. Popular apps like Mint,

PocketGuard, and YNAB (You Need A Budget) are designed to help you manage your money better by tracking every penny you earn and spend.

The benefits of using budgeting apps are pretty cool. One major perk is real-time tracking. You can see exactly where your money goes as soon as you spend it—bought a comic book? It shows up instantly in your app. This helps you stay on top of your spending and avoid surprises. Another benefit is the financial insights these apps offer. They analyze your spending habits and show you where you might be overspending. Maybe you didn't realize you were spending so much on snacks. The app will highlight this and help you make better decisions.

Getting started with budgeting apps is easy. First, download the app you want to use, like Mint or YNAB. Open the app and follow the steps to set up your account. This often involves entering your email and creating a password. Next, link your bank accounts. The app will guide you through this process, which might include logging into your bank account through the app. Once your accounts are linked, you can start creating budgets. Set up categories like food, entertainment, and savings. Decide how much money you want to allocate to each category. This helps you set limits and stay within your budget.

Tracking your expenses is a crucial part of using budgeting apps. Every time you spend money, enter the transaction into the app. You can categorize each expense to see where your money is going. For example, if you buy a movie ticket, you can categorize it under entertainment. This helps you see how much you spend in each category and make adjustments if needed. The app will also show you how much money you have left in each category, helping you avoid overspending.

There are also kid-friendly budgeting apps that make managing money fun and easy. One great app is Allowance & Chores Bot. This app helps you manage your allowance and chores all in one place. You can set up different chores, assign values to them, and track your earnings. It's a great way to learn about budgeting while keeping track of your responsibilities. Another fantastic app is iAllowance. This app helps you track your allowance, set savings goals, and monitor your progress. You can even set up different accounts for spending, saving, and sharing. It's like having a mini bank on your phone.

Imagine you want to save for a new video game. You can use iAllowance to set a savings goal. Each time you get your allowance or complete a chore, you log it in the app. You can see your savings grow and track how close you are to reaching your goal. Allowance & Chores Bot works similarly. You can set up chores like washing the dishes or mowing the lawn. Each time you complete a chore, you earn money and log it in the app. It helps you stay motivated and see the rewards of your hard work.

Budgeting apps are like having a personal finance assistant in your pocket. They help you track your spending, set budgets, and reach your financial goals. These apps allow you to take control of your money and make smarter financial decisions. So next time you wonder where all your allowance went, just check your app. It will show you exactly where your money is going and help you stay on track.

## 6.4 THE IMPORTANCE OF ONLINE SECURITY: PROTECTING YOUR INFORMATION

Imagine you're out and about, and you lose your wallet. Not only would you lose your cash, but also your ID and credit cards. Now,

picture this happening online, but instead of losing your wallet, someone steals your info. That's why online security is so crucial. When someone steals your personal information, it's called **identity theft**. This can lead to trouble, like someone opening credit cards in your name or even taking out loans. You might only know it's happening once you start getting bills for things you never bought.

Another significant risk is **financial fraud**. This happens when someone gets access to your bank accounts or credit cards and starts spending your money. Imagine checking your bank account and finding out your money is gone. It's a scary thought, but it happens more often than you think. Protecting your personal and financial information online is key to preventing these issues.

So, how can you keep your information safe? Start with robust and unique passwords. A **strong password** is hard to guess and uses a mix of letters, numbers, and symbols. Avoid using obvious things like your name, birthday, or "password123." Instead, try something like "P@ssw0rd$ecure!" The more random, the better. Also, don't use the same password for multiple accounts. If one gets hacked, all your accounts could be at risk.

Another good practice is to **avoid public Wi-Fi**. Public Wi-Fi networks are usually not secure, making it easy for hackers to intercept your data. If you must use public Wi-Fi, avoid accessing sensitive accounts like your bank. Always use a secure network or your mobile data. Regularly updating your software and apps is also important. Updates often include security fixes that protect against new threats. Make it a habit to check for updates and install them as soon as they're available.

Online threats come in many forms. **Phishing scams** are one of the most common. These are fraudulent emails that look like they come from a trusted source, like your bank. They usually ask for personal information or prompt you to click a link. If you do, you could end up giving away your info or downloading malware. Always be cautious with emails that ask for personal information. Look for signs of phishing, like poor grammar, strange email addresses, and urgent requests for action.

**Malware** is another significant threat. This is malicious software designed to harm your computer or steal your information. It can come from downloading files, clicking on bad links, or visiting certain websites. To prevent malware:

1. Use antivirus software and keep it updated.
2. Be careful about what you download and where you click.
3. Only download files from trusted sources, and avoid clicking on pop-ups or suspicious links.

Let's look at a real-life scenario. Meet Alex, a savvy young internet user. One day, Alex gets an email that looks like it's from his favorite online game. The email says he needs to update his account info, or it will be deleted. It looks official, but Alex remembers learning about phishing scams. He checks the email address and notices it's slightly different from the real one. Instead of clicking the link in the email, Alex goes directly to the game's website and logs in. There's no message about updating his info. Alex avoids falling for the scam and keeps his account safe.

Using **password managers** can also help keep your information secure. These tools store your passwords securely and can generate strong passwords for you. It's like having a digital vault for all your passwords. You only need to remember one master password to access the manager. This way, you can have unique and strong passwords for all your accounts without the hassle of remembering them all.

Staying safe online doesn't have to be complicated. You can protect your personal and financial information by using strong passwords, avoiding public Wi-Fi, keeping your software updated, and being aware of common threats. Remember, caution goes a long way in keeping your online experiences safe and secure.

## 6.5 FINANCIAL LITERACY WEBSITES: RESOURCES FOR LEARNING

Imagine sitting in your room, laptop open, learning about money without going anywhere. That's the beauty of financial literacy websites. These sites offer educational content on economic topics. They are like virtual classrooms where you can learn about money, budgeting, saving, and investing. Websites like Investopedia, Khan Academy, and Practical Money Skills, among others, provide a wealth of information. They break down complex financial concepts into simple, easy-to-understand lessons. It's like having a personal finance teacher available 24/7, right at your fingertips.

Financial literacy websites are incredibly beneficial. They offer free and comprehensive resources that make learning about money accessible to everyone. You don't need to pay for expensive courses or buy thick textbooks. Everything you need is just a few clicks away. These websites are also interactive. They offer videos, quizzes, articles, and even games to make learning fun and engaging. Imagine watching a video on budgeting your allowance and then taking a quiz to test what you've learned. These interactive features help reinforce your understanding and make learning enjoyable.

Let's look at some top financial literacy websites that are particularly useful for kids and parents. Practical Money Skills is a fantastic resource. It offers games and lessons on money management. You can play games like Financial Football to learn about budgeting and saving while having fun. Another great website is Biz Kid$. This site provides financial education videos specifically for kids. The videos cover topics like earning, saving, spending, and investing. They are entertaining and educational, making it easy to learn about money. MyMoney.gov is another excellent resource. It's a government website dedicated to financial literacy. It offers various resources, from articles and worksheets to interactive tools and games. It's a reliable source of information for both kids and parents.

Using these resources effectively involves a few key steps. First, set learning goals. Decide what you want to learn. You may want to understand how to create a budget or learn about investing. Having specific goals helps you stay focused and motivated. Next, engage in interactive activities. Don't just read the articles or watch the videos. Take the quizzes, play the games, and do the exercises. These activities reinforce what you've learned and make the information stick. Lastly, involve your family. Learning about money can be a fun family activity. Parents and kids can explore the content together, discuss what they've learned, and even set up family challenges or goals. This makes learning about money a shared experience that benefits everyone.

Imagine you and your family sitting down one evening and exploring Practical Money Skills. You decide to play a game together. You choose Financial Football, where you answer questions about money to advance on the field. Each correct answer helps your team move closer to scoring a touchdown. You discuss the answers, learn new concepts, and have a blast together. Next, you watch a Biz Kid$ video on saving money. You learn the importance of saving a part of your allowance instead of spending it all. You discuss how you can apply what you've learned to your own allowance. Finally, you can visit MyMoney.gov to find tools and worksheets. You use these to create a family budget and set savings goals. Each family member has a goal, and you work together to achieve it.

Financial literacy websites are a treasure trove of information and resources. They make learning about money easy, fun, and accessible. You can make the most of these resources by setting learning goals, engaging with interactive activities, and involving your family. Whether playing games, watching videos, or using tools, these websites help you better understand and manage your money. So grab your laptop or tablet, gather your family, and start exploring the wonderful world of financial literacy websites.

Here are some other great financial literacy websites where kids and parents can learn about money, budgeting, saving, and investing:

Money Confident Kids (by T. Rowe Price) offers interactive activities, quizzes, and resources to help parents teach their children the importance of saving, smart spending, and investing. It's designed to make learning about money fun and approachable for kids.

Jump$tart Coalition promotes financial literacy for children and young adults. The site provides links to numerous financial education resources, guides for educators, and a clearinghouse of tools for teaching personal finance at different age levels.

The Mint (by Northwestern Mutual) offers practical advice and activities for kids, teens, parents, and teachers. It covers topics like saving, budgeting, investing, and understanding credit, with a special section for parents to teach money management skills to their children.

NGPF (Next Gen Personal Finance) (https://www.ngpf.org) is a platform that provides a free, up-to-date personal finance curriculum for educators. It's also a valuable resource for parents and kids. It covers various financial topics, from budgeting and saving to investing and managing credit, with interactive games and lessons.

Smart About Money (SAM) provides free articles, calculators, and courses for people of all ages. It's an excellent resource for parents and teens looking to understand personal finance better.

## 6.6 SETTING UP PARENTAL CONTROLS: SAFE DIGITAL PRACTICES

Think of parental controls as your digital safety net. Imagine you're in a playground full of exciting things, but some are too risky. Parental controls help keep you safe while you explore. Setting up these controls is super essential for keeping kids safe online. They allow

parents to monitor what their kids are doing, restrict access to inappropriate content, and set limits on screen time. This way, kids can enjoy the fun parts of the internet without stumbling into places they shouldn't be.

Setting up parental controls on devices like smartphones and tablets is pretty straightforward. Most devices come with built-in features that are easy to activate. On an **iPhone** or **iPad**, go to Settings, then Screen Time, and tap

"Turn On Screen Time." Follow the prompts to set a passcode. Parents can then set app limits, block inappropriate content, and schedule downtime. For **Android** devices, go to Settings, then Digital Wellbeing & Parental Controls. Follow the steps to set up a Family Link account. This lets parents control app usage, set screen time limits, and monitor activity.

You can set up controls for computers on both browsers and operating systems. On a **Windows** computer, go to Settings, then Accounts, and click Family & Other Users. Add a family member and follow the prompts to set up parental controls. You can block websites, set screen time limits, and monitor activity. On a **Mac**, go to System Preferences, then Screen Time. Turn on Screen Time and set up controls for different users. For browsers like Chrome, you can use extensions like "BlockSite" to restrict access to specific websites.

Gaming consoles also come with parental control options. On a **PlayStation**, go to Settings, then Parental Controls/Family Management. You can set game age limits, restrict communication with other players, and set playtime limits. For **Xbox**, go to Settings, then Account, and click Family Settings. Here you can manage app and game restrictions, set screen time limits, and control online interactions. These settings help ensure that gaming stays fun and safe.

There are also great parental control apps and tools. **Qustodio** is a popular choice. It offers screen time management, app blocking, and activity monitoring features. Parents can see what kids do online and set limits to keep them focused. **Net Nanny** is another comprehensive tool. Parents can block inappropriate content, manage screen time, and monitor social media activity. These apps provide peace of mind, knowing kids are safely exploring the digital world.

Maintaining safe digital practices is an ongoing task. Regular check-ins are crucial. Sit down with your kids and discuss their online activity. Ask them what websites they visit, what games they play, and who they talk to. This keeps the lines of communication open and helps you stay informed. Educating kids about safe online behavior is also crucial. Teach them never to share personal information like their name, address, or phone number. Explain the importance of respecting others online and not engaging in cyberbullying. Encourage them to come to you if they encounter anything that makes them uncomfortable.

A practical tip is to set up a family agreement for online behavior. This can include rules about screen time, acceptable websites, and what to do if they see something inappropriate. Having clear guidelines helps everyone stay on the same page. Another tip is to use technology to your advantage. Many devices and apps offer features like activity reports and alerts. Use these tools to stay informed and make adjustments as needed.

Other highly-rated and widely-used parental control apps and tools, similar to Qustodio and Net Nanny, are **Bark**, which monitors texts, emails, and social media for potential risks, such as cyberbullying, inappropriate content, and online predators. It also offers screen time management and web filtering. **FamilyTime** allows parents to manage their children's screen time, set app limits, block inappropriate content, and track their location. **Kaspersky Safe Kids** offers robust parental controls, including web filtering, app management, and real-time GPS tracking, with easy-to-use features.

These apps are among the most trusted and frequently used by parents to ensure safe online experiences for their children.

In summary, parental controls are your digital safety net. They help keep kids safe while they enjoy the internet. Setting them up on smartphones, tablets, computers, and gaming consoles is easy and provides peace of mind. Using these apps adds an extra layer of protection. Regular check-ins and educating kids about safe online behavior are essential for maintaining a positive digital environment. So, use these tools and tips and dive into the digital world safely and confidently.

## 6.7 DIGITAL CURRENCY: BALANCING INNOVATION WITH CAUTION

Digital currencies have captured global attention, offering exciting possibilities in the financial world. From Bitcoin to Ethereum and beyond, these digital assets have the potential to reshape how we think about money. But in the rush to embrace this new technology, it's vital to avoid a "utopian" mindset that overlooks potential risks. In these lines, we'll take a closer look at the history of digital currencies, their pros and cons, and how they compare to traditional money, including the emergence of digital versions of fiat currencies.

### A Brief History of Digital Currencies

The concept of digital currencies started with Bitcoin in 2009, created by an anonymous person known as Satoshi Nakamoto. Bitcoin was the first decentralized cryptocurrency designed to allow peer-to-peer transactions without the need for banks or government control. Since then, thousands of other cryptocurrencies have emerged, each with its own features and goals. Ethereum, for instance, presented the concept of smart contracts—self-executing contracts that automatically enforce the terms of an agreement, cutting out the need for intermediaries like banks or lawyers.

## Pros of Digital Currencies

### 1. Financial Inclusion

One of the most promising aspects of digital currencies is their potential to provide financial access to people who traditional banks underserve. In many developing countries, access to banking services is limited, but smartphones and internet connectivity are becoming more widespread. Digital currencies allow people to store, send, and receive money without needing a physical bank account.

### 2. Faster, Cheaper Transactions

Cross-border payments, which can take days through traditional banking systems, are much faster with digital currencies. The decentralized feature of blockchain technology enables transactions to occur almost instantly without the hefty fees typically associated with international transfers, making digital currencies appealing for personal and business use.

### 3. Greater Control Over Personal Assets

Unlike fiat currency in a bank account, digital currencies give users complete control over their funds. There's no intermediary between you and your money, which can be especially appealing in regions with unstable financial systems or government restrictions on personal wealth.

### 4. Decentralization and Transparency

Digital currencies are built on blockchain technology, which is decentralized and transparent. This means that no single entity, like a bank or government, controls the currency. Transactions are recorded in a public ledger, making them difficult to tamper with and increasing transparency. This has been a critical selling point for those distrusting traditional financial systems.

## 6.8 DIGITAL VERSIONS OF FIAT CURRENCIES

In recent years, even governments and central banks have started exploring digital currencies. Central Bank Digital Currencies (CBDCs) are digital versions of fiat money, such as the U.S. dollar or the Euro. Countries like China, Sweden, and the Bahamas have launched or are testing their own CBDCs. These digital equivalents of fiat currencies aim to combine the stability of traditional money with the convenience and speed of digital transactions. Unlike decentralized cryptocurrencies like Bitcoin, CBDCs are fully backed and regulated by central authorities.

CBDCs could make payment systems more efficient and inclusive. However, they also raise questions about privacy and government oversight, as these digital currencies allow for real-time transaction tracking.

**Cons and Risks of Digital Currencies**

**1. Price Volatility**

One of the most significant drawbacks of many digital currencies is their extreme price volatility. While Bitcoin and other cryptocurrencies have seen dramatic value increases, they've also experienced sharp crashes, wiping out significant amounts of wealth in short periods. For investors, this volatility can make digital currencies highly speculative and risky.

**2. Security Risks**

Digital wallets, which are used to store cryptocurrencies, can be hacked. And because transactions are irreversible, stolen funds are almost impossible to recover. Additionally, you could lose your funds permanently if you lose access to your digital wallet—through a forgotten password or misplaced private key.

**3. Regulation and Legal Uncertainty**

The regulatory environment for digital currencies is still developing, which leads to uncertainty. Governments worldwide have taken different stances on cryptocurrencies, from complete acceptance to outright bans. This patchwork of regulations can make it challenging to know where you legally stand when using or investing in digital assets.

**4. Environmental Impact**

The process of "mining" certain cryptocurrencies, like Bitcoin, requires enormous computational power and energy. This has led to concerns about the environmental impact of cryptocurrency mining, particularly given the global push to reduce carbon emissions.

### Proceed with Caution

While digital currencies offer exciting possibilities, they are not without risk. The promise of faster transactions, greater financial access, and control over personal assets must be weighed against the potential downsides—volatility, security risks, and environmental costs. Additionally, the rise of Central Bank Digital Currencies (CBDCs) introduces an extra level of complexity, as they bring the benefits of digital transactions but also raise concerns about privacy and government control.

Before considering any investment in digital currencies, thoroughly research the specific assets you're interested in. Avoid being swept up in the hype, and ensure you understand the rewards and risks. As with any financial decision, informed

# 7

# CREDIT AND DEBT:

## UNDERSTANDING BORROWING

Imagine you're at the store and see a toy you've wanted for months. You don't have enough money, but the store offers to let you take it home if you promise to pay later. This is the basic idea of credit. It's like borrowing money to buy something now and agreeing to pay it back later. Credit can be a powerful tool but comes with responsibilities and costs. Let's explore what credit means and how it works.

### 7.1 WHAT IS CREDIT? SIMPLE DEFINITIONS

Credit is when you borrow money that you promise to pay back later. Think of it as a loan. When you borrow money, you get to use it immediately, but then you need to return the same amount, plus a little extra called interest. Understanding borrowing and repayment is key. If you borrow $100, you must pay back the $100 along with any interest.

Trust and creditworthiness are crucial in borrowing. Lenders need to trust that you'll pay back the money. Your creditworthiness is like your financial reputation. It shows lenders how reliable you are when it comes to repaying loans. Lenders trust you more if you consistently pay back what you owe on time.

Interest is the cost of borrowing money. You have to pay back more than you borrowed when you borrow money. That extra money is called interest. It's how lenders make money from lending. For example, if you borrow $100 with 5% interest, you will pay back $105. That's $100 you borrowed plus $5 interest. Interest payments can add up, so it's essential to understand how much you'll owe in total.

There are **different types of credit**. Credit cards are a common type. They offer a revolving line of credit with a borrowing limit. This means you can borrow up to a certain amount, repay it, and borrow again. Loans are another form of credit. They are fixed-term borrowing for specific purposes, like buying a car or going to college. You borrow a set amount and pay it back over time with interest. Store credit is credit offered by retail stores. They let you buy items now and pay for them later, often with interest. Each type of credit has its own rules and costs.

Credit plays a paramount role in the economy. It supports consumer spending, which is when people buy items on credit. This spending helps businesses grow because more people can buy their products. Businesses also use credit to expand. They borrow money to open new stores, hire more workers, or buy new equipment. For example, people often use credit when buying homes or cars. They get a loan to buy a house or car and then pay it back over time. This allows people to make big purchases they couldn't afford to pay for all at once.

The credit helps you buy things now and pay for them later. But it also means you must be responsible and repay what you owe. Understanding how credit works, the types of credit available, and the role of interest will help you use credit wisely. Whether you're using a credit card, taking out a loan, or buying something on store credit, knowing the basics of credit can help you make intelligent financial decisions.

## 7.2 USING CREDIT WISELY: DOS AND DON'TS

Using credit wisely starts with understanding some important **dos**. First, always pay on time. When you borrow money, you agree to pay it back by a specific date. Missing this date can lead to extra fees and damage your credit. Setting up payment reminders on your devices can help you stay on track. You can use a calendar, an app, or sticky notes on your fridge. Another smart move is to borrow within limits. This means only using a small portion of your available credit. If you have a credit limit of $1,000, try not to spend more than $300. This keeps your borrowing manageable and shows lenders you can handle credit responsibly.

Regularly monitoring your statements is also crucial. Each month, you'll get a credit card statement that shows how much you owe and when your payment is due. Checking this statement helps you spot any mistakes or unauthorized charges. It also lets you see where your money is going. You may cut back if you notice you're spending a lot at your favorite coffee shop. Setting up alerts through your credit card's mobile app can make this even easier. These alerts can notify you of due dates, large purchases, or low balances.

Now, let's talk about the **don'ts** of using credit. Overspending is a common mistake. It's easy to swipe your card without considering how much you spend. However, high balances can lead to significant interest charges and make it hard to pay off your debt. Try to stick to a budget and avoid buying things you don't need. Ignoring your statements is another big no-no. If you don't review your monthly statements, you might miss errors or forget to make a payment. This can lead to late fees and a lower credit score. Skipping payments is the worst mistake. Missing even one payment can hurt your credit score and lead to higher interest rates. Always make at least the minimum payment on time.

Using credit wisely comes with many **benefits**. One of the biggest is building a good credit history. This is like a report card for your borrowing habits. A favorable credit history shows lenders that you're reliable, making it easier to get loans or credit cards in the future when you want to make big purchases like buying a house or a car. You'll also get access to better terms, like lower interest rates and higher credit limits. This means you'll pay less interest and have more borrowing power when needed.

Let's look at some real-life scenarios to see how these practices work. Take the story of Emily, a teen who got her first credit card at 18. She used it sparingly, only for small purchases like gas and groceries. She set up payment reminders and always paid her bills on time. Over time, she built a solid credit history. When she applied for a car loan a few years later, she got a low interest rate because of her good credit. On the flip side, there's Jake, who got his first credit card and went on a spending spree. He maxed out his card and ignored his statements. Soon, he was overwhelmed by debt and missed several payments. His credit score plummeted, making it hard for him to get loans or rent an apartment.

Using credit wisely means making wise choices. Pay on time, borrow within limits, and check your statements. Avoid overspending, ignoring your statements, and skipping payments. By following these simple guidelines, you can enjoy the benefits of credit without the stress.

**Interactive WhatsApp Group Activity: "Smart Credit Challenge"**

This fun and engaging activity helps parents and kids learn and practice intelligent credit habits through real-life scenarios. You'll create a WhatsApp group for the family and complete challenges together. The aim is to reinforce critical concepts like paying on time, borrowing within limits, checking statements, and avoiding overspending.

**Instructions:**

1. **Create a WhatsApp group** for the family (parents and kids).
2. **Name the group** something fun like "**Smart Credit Masters.**"
3. Each day, send a scenario to the group where the family members must respond with what they would do. Points are awarded for correct answers. Track points over the week to see who earns the title of "Credit Master."

**Day 1: Scenario - Pay on Time**

**Message in the group:**

*"You have a credit card payment due in 3 days, but you just found out your favorite game is on sale today. You really want to buy it. What do you do?"*

**Options**:

a. Buy the game and pay the credit card bill later.
b. Pay the credit card bill first, then see if you can afford the game.

c. Ignore both and hope for the best!

**Answer:** b. Pay the credit card bill first.

**Discussion**: Paying on time is essential to avoid late fees and penalties. If you manage your money well, you can still get that game!

**Day 2: Scenario - Borrow Within Limits**

**Message in the group:**

*"You're planning to buy a new bike, and you have a credit limit of $1,000. The bike costs $800, but you must also pay $300 in other bills this month. What do you do?"*

**Options**:

a. Buy the bike now and deal with the bills later.
b. Pay the bills first and save more before buying the bike.
c. Increase your credit limit and get the bike today.

**Answer:** b) Pay the bills first.

**Discussion**: Borrowing within limits helps avoid debt. It's better to wait and save than max out your credit limit.

**Day 3: Scenario - Check Your Statement**

**Message in the group:**

*"You get your credit card statement and see a charge you don't remember making. What should you do?"*

**Options**:

a. Ignore it; it's probably nothing.
b. Check your receipts and contact your credit card company if it's an error.
c. Wait a month and see if it fixes itself.

**Answer:** b) Check receipts and contact the company.

**Discussion**: Always check your statement for errors or fraud. Quickly contacting your credit card company can help fix problems before they grow.

**Day 4: Scenario - Avoid Overspending**

**Message in the group:**

*"You just got your allowance and see a new gadget that costs $300. Your budget only allows for $100 this month. What do you do?"*

**Options**:

a. Use your credit card to buy it anyway.
b. Wait until you save up more money to buy it.
c. Borrow money from a friend to buy it.

**Answer:** b) Wait until you can afford it.

**Discussion**: Overspending on credit can lead to significant debt later. It's smarter to wait until you can afford the gadget with your budget.

**Day 5: Scenario - Ignoring Statements and Skipping Payments**

**Message in the group:**

*"You forgot to check your credit card statement last month and missed a payment. You have a lot of schoolwork this month and might not have time to check again. What do you do?"*

**Options**:

a. Ignore it and hope you remember next month.
b. Set a reminder on your phone to pay on time.
c. skip the payment until you feel less busy.

**Answer:** b) Set a reminder to pay on time.

**Discussion**: Skipping payments can lead to late fees and hurt your credit score. Setting up reminders can help you stay on track.

**Bonus Round - Role Play!**

**Message in the group:**

*"Let's role-play! One person pretends to be the credit card company; the other is the customer who missed a payment. Discuss what happens and how the customer can fix it."*

**Wrap-up:**

At the end of the week, count the points. Whoever has the most points becomes the "**Smart Credit Master**" for the week. The family should discuss what they learned about using credit wisely and how they can apply these lessons in real life!

## 7.3 UNDERSTANDING DEBT: THE RISKS AND CONSEQUENCES

Before diving into this topic, let's start with this fun and interactive game. The goal is to spark conversation and make learning fun. Our WhatsApp group will now change to Debt Detective!

"Welcome to Debt Detective! We're going to investigate some mysterious money-related situations, and your answers will help us solve the case! Are you ready?"

**Message:** *"Imagine you've borrowed some money and suddenly realize you don't have enough to pay it back. How do you think you'd feel?"*

Topic: Financial Stress & Damaged Credit Score

**Message:** *"What would you do if you had to pay back $200 each month but only had $150 left after covering your expenses?"*

Topic: Budgeting for Repayments

**Message:** *"If you already owe money, would it be a good idea to borrow more to buy something new you want? Why or why not?"*

Topic: Avoiding New Debt

**Message:** *"Imagine you owe money to three different people. What would you do to make things easier?"*

Topic: Consolidating Debt

**Message:** *"If you had a lot of debt, how do you think you could create a plan to pay it all off over time?"*

Topic: Creating a Debt Repayment Plan

**Message:** *"Debt can be scary, but can you think of any situation where it might be helpful or necessary?"*

Topic: Debt as a Useful Tool

Answers could take a day or two; once all questions have been answered and discussed, we'll use them to introduce the key topics of this chapter:

**Debt** is money you owe to someone else. Think of it as borrowing money with the promise to pay it back later. When you borrow money, you have to repay it, usually with some extra called interest. This extra amount is the cost of borrowing. If you borrow $100 with 5% interest, you will repay $105. Borrowing money means you use it immediately, but you must plan how to repay it.

Debt grows over time because of interest. If you don't pay back what you owe quickly, the interest makes the debt bigger. Imagine a leaky faucet dripping into a bucket. At first, it's just a few drops, but over time, the water fills the bucket, and soon it's overflowing, creating a mess that's difficult to clean up. That's what happens to debt if you don't manage it well. You start with a small amount, but it can become a huge problem if left unchecked.

The consequences of excessive debt can be severe. Financial stress is one of the most significant impacts. When you have too much debt, it can feel overwhelming. You might worry about how to make payments and still have enough money for other needs. This stress can affect your well-being and even your health. Another consequence is a damaged credit score. A credit score is comparable to a report card that reflects how effectively you handle debt. Your score goes down if you have too much debt or miss payments. This makes it harder to borrow money in the future.

Imagine a family struggling with high credit card debt. They bought many things on credit, thinking they could pay it off later. But the interest kept adding up, and now they owe much more than they borrowed. They have to cut back on other expenses to make payments, causing stress and tension at home. This shows how easily debt can spiral out of control if not managed properly.

Responsibly managing debt is crucial. One strategy is **budgeting for repayments**. This means setting aside money each month specifically to pay off debt. Create a budget that includes your income and expenses, making sure to allocate enough for debt payments. **Avoiding new debt** is another important step. Concentrate on repaying your existing debt before considering taking on additional obligations. This helps you get back on track without adding to the problem.

**Consolidating debt** can also be a helpful strategy. This means combining multiple debts into one manageable payment. For example, if you have several credit card debts, you might take a loan to pay them off. Then, you only have one loan to focus on, often with a lower interest rate. This makes it easier to manage and can save you money in the long run.

Real-life examples can illustrate the importance of managing debt wisely. Let's look at the story of John. He had several credit card debts and struggled to keep up with payments. He decided to create a debt repayment plan. John listed all his debts, their interest rates, and minimum payments. He focused on paying off the debt with the highest interest rate first while doing minimum payments on the others. Once John had paid off the first debt, he moved on to the next one. Over time, he cleared all his debts. This method is often called the "avalanche method."

A practical tip for managing debt is to set a **debt repayment plan**. List all your debts, including the amounts, interest rates, and minimum payments. Prioritize which debts to pay off first. Some people prefer to tackle the smallest debts first for quick wins, known as the "snowball method." Like John, others focus on the highest interest rates to save money. Whichever method you choose, stick to your plan and track your progress.

On the other hand, debt can also be a **helpful tool** when used wisely! For example, many successful businessmen and women borrow money to start or grow their businesses. They use loans or credit to buy equipment, hire people, or expand their services, knowing they can pay it back later as their business grows. The key is only to borrow what you need and to have a plan to pay it back on time. Like a tool, debt can help you build something great, but you must use it carefully!

Borrowing money means repaying it, usually with interest. Too much debt can cause significant financial stress and a damaged credit score. You can manage debt responsibly by budgeting for repayments, avoiding new debt, and considering consolidation. Real-life examples and practical tips can guide you in making intelligent choices.

## 7.4 CREDIT CARDS FOR KIDS: SAFE PRACTICES

Imagine you're a teen wanting to buy something online but don't have cash or a debit card. This is where credit cards come in. Credit cards can be an excellent tool for teens to learn about managing money, but they must be used responsibly. One safe way to start is with **prepaid cards**. These work like credit cards but are loaded with a fixed amount. You can only spend the amount on the card, making it a good starting point for learning credit management.

Another option is becoming an **authorized user** on a parent's credit card. This means your name is added to the card, and you can use it to make purchases. However, the primary cardholder (usually your parent) is responsible for paying the bill. This setup helps you learn to use credit while having a safety net. It's like having training wheels on a bike. You get the experience of managing credit, but your parent is there to guide you and ensure you stay caught up.

Starting early with credit cards has several benefits. One significant advantage is building a good **credit history**. When you use credit responsibly, you show lenders you can be trusted to repay your debts. This helps you establish a favorable credit record, making it easier to get loans or credit cards in the future. Another benefit is learning **financial responsibility**. Using a credit card teaches you how to manage spending and payments. You learn to track your expenses, make timely payments, and stay within your budget.

There are some important practices to follow when using a credit card responsibly. First, **keep track of your spending**. Regularly monitor your transactions to see where your money is going. This helps you avoid overspending and catch any unauthorized charges. **Paying your balance in full** each month is another crucial practice. This means paying off the entire amount you owe, not just the minimum payment. By doing this, you avoid interest charges and keep your debt under control. **Setting spending limits** is also important. Decide how much you can afford each month and stick to that limit. This contributes to you staying within your budget and avoiding accumulating debt.

Using a budgeting app can make tracking your credit card expenses easier. These apps help you set budgets, track spending, and remind you of payment due dates. For example, you can set a budget for different categories like food, entertainment, and transportation. The app will show you how much you've spent in each category and how much you have left. This keeps you informed and helps you make better spending decisions.

Let's look at some success stories of teens who used credit cards responsibly. Sarah was added as an authorized user on her mom's credit card when she turned 16. Her mom explained how to use the card wisely and set spending limits. Sarah used the card for school supplies and small purchases. She tracked her spending using a budgeting app and always paid her balance in full. By the time she turned 18, she had built a strong credit history, making it easier for her to get her credit card with favorable terms.

Another practical tip for managing credit cards is **setting up automatic payments**. This ensures that your credit card bill is paid on time every month, reducing the risk of late fees and interest charges. You can set up automatic payments through your bank or credit card provider. Just make sure you have enough money in your account to cover the payment. This practice helps you avoid missed payments and keeps your credit score in good shape.

Credit cards can be a valuable tool for kids to learn about financial responsibility. Starting with prepaid cards or becoming an authorized user on a parent's card provides a safe way to gain experience. The benefits of early starting include building a good credit history and learning to manage spending and payments. Kids can use credit cards wisely by keeping track of spending, paying balances in total, and setting spending limits. Success stories like Sarah's show that with the proper practices, kids can manage credit responsibly and set themselves up for a solid financial future.

## 7.5 THE IMPORTANCE OF A GOOD CREDIT SCORE: HOW IT AFFECTS YOU

A credit score serves as your financial report card, reflecting your money management habits. It's a number that shows how good you are at managing borrowed money. The most common model

is the FICO score. This score ranges from 300 to 850. A low score means you need to improve at paying back what you owe. A high score means you are reliable and pay back loans on time. Most people aim for a score above 700. This is considered good and can open many financial doors for you.

Several factors influence your credit score. One of the biggest is your payment history. If you consistently pay your bills on time, your score goes up. When you miss a payment, your score can drop. Another important factor is credit utilization. This is the ratio of how much credit you use compared to how much you have available. If you have a credit limit of $1,000 and use $200, your utilization is 20%. Keeping this ratio low, ideally below 30%, helps your score. The length of your credit history also matters. The longer you've had credit accounts, the better. Having multiple accounts open for a long time can boost your score. But opening too many new accounts in a short period can hurt it. Lenders see this as risky behavior.

Maintaining a high credit score comes with many benefits. One of the biggest is getting better loan terms. This means lower interest rates and higher credit limits. Imagine you are buying a house. With a high credit score, you could get a lower mortgage rate. This means you pay less interest over the life of the loan, saving you thousands of dollars. Easier approval is another benefit. When you apply for credit cards or loans, a high score increases your chances of getting approved. Lenders see you as a low-risk borrower.

Let's look at an example. Janet has a high credit score of 750. She applies for a mortgage to buy her first home. Because of her good score, she gets a low interest rate, which saves her a lot of money over the years. On the flip side, Jake has a low score of 600. He gets a higher interest rate when he applies for the same mortgage. He ends up paying much more in interest over the life of the loan.

Improving and maintaining a good credit score is possible with some practical steps. First, always pay your bills on time. Schedule reminders or enable automatic payments to ensure you never miss a deadline. Keeping your balances low is another critical practice. Try to use only a small portion of your available credit. If you have a $1,000 limit, aim to use no more than $300. This keeps your credit utilization low and helps your score. Regularly monitoring your credit report is also essential. Check for errors or fraudulent activities that could hurt your score. You can get a free credit report from each of the three major credit bureaus once a year: Equifax, Experian, and TransUnion.

Following these steps can help you build and maintain a good credit score. This opens many financial opportunities, from better loan terms to easier credit approval. It's like having a passport that lets you confidently and easily explore the world of finance.

## 7.6 AVOIDING DEBT TRAPS: SMART BORROWING TIPS

What if you needed money immediately, but the loan would cost you much more later? Would you still take it or try to find another way?

Have you ever agreed to something without reading all the details? What could happen if you did that with a loan?"

Can borrowing money ever be an intelligent choice? How could borrowing help you if done the right way?

Debt traps are financial pitfalls that can be tough to escape. They lure you in with seemingly easy money but come with hidden dangers. High-interest debt is one of these traps. Imagine borrowing $100 and having to pay back $120. That extra $20 is the high interest, making the loan very costly. Payday loans are another example. They are short-term loans with high fees and interest rates. People often use them to cover emergencies, but the high costs can trap them in a cycle of debt.

Debt traps can be harmful for many reasons. They make paying off the borrowed amount challenging, leading to more borrowing. This creates a vicious cycle of borrowing to pay off previous loans, increasing your debt over time. For instance, someone might take a payday loan to fix a car, but the high fees and interest make it difficult to repay. They might take another loan to cover the first, leading to more debt. This cycle can be stressful and hard to break.

You need to recognize and steer clear of debt traps to avoid them. Start by reading the terms and conditions of any loan agreement. Understand the interest rates, fees, and repayment terms. Avoid impulsive borrowing. Think carefully before taking on debt. Do you really need the loan? Can you afford the repayments? Calculate the total repayment costs before borrowing. For example, if you borrow $500 with high interest, you might end up paying back $700. Knowing this upfront helps you make informed decisions.

Safer borrowing options can help you meet your financial needs without falling into debt traps. Personal loans from banks or credit unions typically offer lower interest rates and more manageable terms than payday loans. They are a better option for borrowing money. Borrowing from family is another alternative. Family members might offer interest-free or low-interest loans.

Just make sure to agree on repayment terms to avoid misunderstandings.

Smart borrowing involves practical strategies to manage debt responsibly. Borrow within limits. Only take on debt that you can repay comfortably. Planning for repayment is crucial. Create a repayment plan before borrowing. Know how much you must pay monthly and ensure you can meet those payments. Using a loan calculator can help. It shows you the monthly payments and total repayment costs, helping you plan better.

Debt traps can be sneaky, but you can avoid them with careful planning and smart choices. Whether considering a loan or finding alternatives, always consider the long-term impact on your finances. By understanding the dangers, recognizing traps, and choosing safer options, you can borrow money responsibly and stay out of trouble.

Debt is a helpful tool when managed wisely. However, falling into debt traps can create financial stress and make it hard to achieve your goals. By borrowing smartly, reading loan terms, and planning repayments, you can use debt to your advantage without falling into traps. Understanding these principles sets a strong foundation for managing money.

This chapter on credit and debt gives you the tools to make informed financial decisions. As we move on, we'll explore more ways to build a solid financial future.

## 7.7 A HEARTFELT CONVERSATION ABOUT GIVING BACK: PHILANTHROPY AND FINANCIAL RESPONSIBILITY

Now that we've learned about intelligent money management, let's have a different kind of conversation—about something just as important: giving back. It's not just about what we earn or save but how we can use our resources to help others and make the world a better place. Let's explore how being financially responsible also means being generous and thoughtful about how we share.

Once, while I was helping with a food drive at a fraternal organization, all the members agreed to bring food for people in need. When my daughter found out, she asked me, 'Why don't some people have enough food to eat?' That simple question opened my eyes to how important it is to teach kids about giving back. It's not just about handing over money; it's about understanding the struggles others face, showing kindness, and making the world better. So, let's explore the outstanding world of giving and why it matters so much for all of us.

## 7.8 THE JOY OF GIVING: WHY PHILANTHROPY MATTERS

Philanthropy might sound like a big word, but it's just about helping others and positively impacting the world. The word philanthropy is derived from Ancient Greek phílos (φίλος), "who loves," and ánthrôpos (ἄνθρωπος), "humankind." Thus, philanthropy means "love for humanity."

It's about giving your time, money, or skills to help people who need it. When you help someone, you're not just improving their life; you're also making your community stronger. Imagine a neighborhood where everyone helps each other. It would be a happier, safer, and more connected place.

Helping others can be as simple as donating clothes you no longer wear, giving toys to kids who don't have any, or organizing a bake sale to raise money for a local charity. These small acts of kindness add up and make a big difference. When you give, you're not just helping others; you're also helping yourself. Giving brings a sense of purpose and fulfillment that nothing else can match. It's a great way to feel good about yourself and know you're improving the world.

Philanthropy also builds a better society. When people help each other, they create a strong community. This sense of community makes everyone feel included and valued. It's like building a giant puzzle where every piece matters. No matter how small, each person's contribution helps complete the picture. This sense of belonging and teamwork makes communities more resilient and better equipped to face challenges.

Giving also has emotional and social benefits. When you help someone, you feel a sense of joy and satisfaction. It's like a warm hug for your heart. Knowing that you made a difference in someone's life gives you a sense of purpose. It also helps you build connections with others. Helping out at a local food bank, joining a community clean-up, or participating in a charity walk are great ways to brighten the world, meet new people, and make friends. These activities strengthen your social network and create a support system you can rely on.

Being socially responsible means recognizing your role in the world and acting in ways that benefit society. It's about knowing how your actions affect others and making choices that contribute to the greater good. For example, recycling, conserving water, and using less plastic are small acts that help protect the environment. Supporting local businesses instead of big chains helps your local economy. Being kind and respectful to others, volunteering your time, and donating to causes you care about are all ways to practice social responsibility.

Are there some fun and simple ways kids can get involved in philanthropy? Sure, yes! Organizing fundraising events is a great start. You can host a bake sale, car wash, or lemonade stand to raise money for a cause you care about. These events are fun and teach you valuable skills like planning, teamwork, and money management. Another way to give back is by donating items you no longer need. Gather clothes, toys, or books in good condition and give them to a local shelter or charity. This helps people in need and gives your old items a new life.

Imagine organizing a bake sale with your friends to raise money for a local animal shelter. You spend the day baking cookies, decorating signs, and selling delicious treats. At the end of the day, you've raised money, had a lot of fun, and learned new skills. Or think about the joy a child feels when they receive a toy they've always wanted. Knowing that you made that possible by donating your old toys can be incredibly rewarding.

Giving back through philanthropy is a meaningful way to create a positive impact on the world. It brings joy, builds strong communities, and teaches valuable life lessons. Whether you're organizing a fundraising event, donating items, or simply being kind and responsible, every act of giving makes a difference. So, let's embrace the joy of giving and work together to make the world a better place.

## 7.9 CHOOSING A CAUSE: HOW TO FIND WHAT YOU CARE ABOUT

Choosing a cause to support might seem like a big task, but it starts with something simple: thinking about what you care about.

Take a moment to reflect on your interests and values. Do you love animals? Are you passionate about the environment? Do you believe everyone should have access to education? Personal reflection helps you connect with causes that truly matter to you. You can start by listing things you love and care about. This can be a fun brainstorm. Write down everything that comes to mind, from protecting wildlife to helping people experiencing homelessness.

Once you have a list, it's time to explore different types of causes. Environmental causes are all about protecting nature and wildlife. This can include planting trees, cleaning up parks, or supporting wildlife conservation efforts. If you care about the planet, this might be the right fit for you. Social causes focus on supporting the underprivileged and marginalized. This can involve helping people without housing, advocating for equal rights, or working to end hunger. If you want to make a difference in people's lives, consider a social cause. Educational causes aim to promote literacy and learning opportunities. This can include tutoring, donating books, or supporting schools in need. If you believe in the power of education, this might be your cause.

Researching and evaluating causes is essential to ensure your efforts have the most impact. Start with online research. Websites like Charity Navigator, GuideStar, and GiveWell can help you find reputable organizations. They provide ratings and reviews to help you assess the effectiveness of different charities. Seek out organizations that share your values and have a proven history of creating meaningful change. Ask questions to understand their mission and how they use donations. For example, if you're interested in supporting an animal shelter, find out how they care for the animals and how your contribution will help.

Let's say you've narrowed down your interests to helping animals. Before you commit, try a volunteering trial. Spend a day at a local animal shelter to see if it's a good fit. This hands-on experience will give you a better understanding of the cause and help you decide if it's something you want to support long-term. You can also create a cause comparison chart. List the causes you're interested in and weigh the pros and cons of each. This visual tool helps you make an informed decision.

**Activity: Cause Comparison Chart**

1. List your top three causes.
2. Write down the pros and cons of each cause.
3. Compare and decide which cause resonates the most with you.
4. Write three to five ideas of what you would do to be involved in your cause.

Imagine you love the ocean and want to protect marine life. You start by researching organizations that focus on marine conservation. You find a reputable charity that organizes beach clean-ups and educates communities about ocean health. You decide to volunteer for a beach clean-up event. After spending the day picking up trash and learning about marine life, you feel a solid connection to the cause. You've found your passion, and you're ready to support it.

Choosing a cause is about finding what matters to you and taking steps to support it. Reflect on your interests, explore different causes, research organizations, and try out volunteer activities. In doing so, you'll find a cause that aligns with your passion and empowers you to make a lasting impact.

## 7.10 VOLUNTEERING AND DONATING: DIFFERENT WAYS TO GIVE

Volunteering and donating are two powerful ways to give back to your community. While both are valuable, they each offer different ways to help others. Volunteering means giving your time and effort to help people or causes. It's about getting involved and making a difference through your actions. For example, you might spend an afternoon cleaning up a park or serving food at a shelter. Donating, on the other hand, involves giving money or items to support a cause. This could mean donating money to a charity or donating clothes and toys to needy people. Both forms of giving significantly impact and show that you care about improving the world.

Volunteering offers many benefits. It helps you learn new skills and gain experiences you might not get otherwise. For instance, volunteering at an animal shelter can teach you how to care for animals, while helping at a food bank can show you how to organize and distribute supplies. These experiences can be fun and rewarding. Volunteering also enables you to build connections and networks within your community. You meet new people, make friends, and become part of a team working towards a common goal. These relationships can be valuable and supportive now and in the future.

There are many ways kids can **volunteer**. Participating in community clean-ups is a great start. You can join local efforts to pick up trash in parks or along roadsides. This helps the environment and makes your community a nicer place to live. Helping at food banks is another excellent opportunity. You can sort and distribute food to those in need, providing a vital service to your community. Volunteering at an animal shelter is also an excellent way to give back. You can help care for animals, clean their living spaces, and even play with them to keep them happy and healthy. These activities not only help others but also provide you with valuable experiences and memories.

**Wisely donating** involves more than just giving away money or items. It's about making thoughtful contributions that genuinely make a difference. Start by choosing reputable and impactful organizations. Research charities to ensure they use donations effectively and align with your values. Websites like Charity Navigator may help you find trustworthy organizations. When donating goods, make sure the items are needed and in good condition. For example, shelters often need clothes, blankets, and toiletries. Schools might need books, supplies, or sports equipment. Planning regular contributions can also make a significant impact. Set donation goals and stick to them, whether giving a portion of your monthly allowance or organizing an annual donation drive.

Imagine you decide to donate some of your toys to a local shelter. First, you sort through your toys and pick the ones you no longer play with but are still in good shape. You clean them up and pack them in a box. Next, you research local shelters to find one that accepts toy donations. You choose a reputable organization and arrange to drop off your donations. The shelter staff are thrilled and explain how your toys will bring joy to the children they support. Knowing that your old toys will make other kids happy is a beautiful feeling.

Volunteering and donating are both fantastic ways to give back. Whether you're spending time helping others or giving away money or items, your contributions matter. They help build stronger communities, support important causes, and provide you with valuable experiences. So, get out there and find the best way to make a difference!

## 7.11 FAMILY GIVING PROJECTS: WORKING TOGETHER TO MAKE A DIFFERENCE

Family giving projects are a fantastic way for families to bond and make a difference. When you work on charitable activities as a family, you strengthen your ties and share essential values. It's more than just giving back. It's about learning responsibility and empathy. Imagine spending a Saturday afternoon collecting items for a local shelter. Everyone pitches in, and you work towards a common goal. These moments create lasting memories and instill a sense of purpose in kids. They learn that even small actions can make a significant impact.

There are many family-giving projects you can try. Charity drives are a great start. You can organize a drive to collect clothes, toys, or canned goods. Each family member can have a role. Someone can make flyers, another can spread the word, and others can help collect and sort donations. **Fundraising** events are also a fun way to get involved. Host a family-run bake sale, car wash, or lemonade stand. These events teach us all about planning, teamwork, and money management. Plus, they're a lot of fun! You can also dedicate a day to community service. **Volunteer** together at a local organization. Whether helping at a food bank or cleaning up a park, you'll work together for a good cause.

One family decided to adopt a local park. They organized regular clean-ups and planted flowers and trees. Every month, they spent a few hours making the park beautiful. This project brought the family closer and improved the quality of life in their community. It's incredible what a collective effort can achieve. When families work together, they combine their skills and resources. Parents set a positive example for their kids, showing them the importance of giving back. Kids learn by watching their parents and feel proud to contribute.

Planning and executing **family-giving projects** doesn't have to be complicated. Start by setting clear goals. Decide what you want to achieve and why it matters. This gives everyone a sense of direction. Then, delegate tasks. Assign roles based on each person's strengths and interests. This makes everyone feel involved and valued. Finally, make sure to celebrate your achievements. Recognize and reward everyone's efforts. Have a small party, go out for ice cream, or share your success with friends and family. Celebrating shows that you appreciate everyone's hard work and encourages future participation.

Imagine planning a family car wash to raise money for a local animal shelter. You start by setting a goal to raise $200. Each family member has a role. One makes posters, another gathers supplies, and everyone helps wash cars. You spend the day working together, having fun, and meeting new people. At the end of the day, you count the money and realize you've raised $250. You feel proud and excited to donate the money to the shelter. Reward yourselves with a treat and share the good news with your friends. This experience teaches valuable lessons and strengthens your family bonds.

Here are some other family-giving project ideas that can inspire a sense of community and giving back:

1. **Neighborhood Cleanup Day**: Organize a family-led event to clean up a local park, beach, or neighborhood area. Invite neighbors to join and make it a regular community event.
2. **Family Donation Challenge**: Set a goal for the family to declutter and donate items like clothes, books, toys, or furniture to local shelters or thrift stores. Make it fun by setting a goal for the number of items to donate.

3. **Adopt a Family for the Holidays**: Participate in programs that allow your family to support a less fortunate family by providing gifts, food, or financial support during the holiday season.
4. **Cook and Serve Meals at a Shelter**: As a family, volunteer to cook and serve meals at a homeless shelter or soup kitchen. It's a hands-on way to give back and interact with the community directly.
5. **Create Care Packages**: Assemble care packages for people in need, such as hygiene kits for shelters, snack packs for kids in foster care, or "blessing bags" with essentials for homeless individuals.
6. **Support a Cause Through Walk-a-thons or Charity Runs**: Join charity walks or runs as a family, raising funds and awareness for causes like cancer research, hunger, or environmental protection.
7. **Sponsor a Child or Animal**: As a family, commit to sponsoring a child through organizations like Save the Children or an animal through wildlife preservation programs. Track their progress and learn together about the impact of your support.
8. **Plant a Community Garden**: Create a small garden in your neighborhood to provide fresh produce for residents, especially in areas with limited access to fresh food. This also teaches sustainability and responsibility.
9. **Host a Charity Garage Sale**: Gather unused items and hold a garage sale, with all proceeds going to a chosen charity. Kids can be involved by letting them sell their toys or baked goods to contribute.
10. **Build with Habitat for Humanity**: If children are old enough, they can participate in a project to help build homes for those in need, teaching valuable life skills and the importance of housing security.

These ideas allow families to bond while meaningfully impacting their community.

Family-giving projects are a powerful way to make a positive impact. They teach kids about responsibility, empathy, and teamwork. They bring families closer and create lasting memories. Whether organizing a charity drive, hosting a fundraising event, or volunteering together, you're making a difference. So, gather your family, pick a project, and start giving back together. It's a journey filled with fun, learning, and lots of heart.

## 7.12 PLANNING CHARITABLE CONTRIBUTIONS: BUDGETING FOR GIVING

Budgeting for charitable giving is like planning for a special event. You want to ensure you have enough to give without running out of money for other things. It's about being financially responsible while making a positive impact. When you plan your giving, you ensure consistency. This means you can make regular and meaningful contributions. Like saving for a new bike, setting aside money for charity helps you give back without feeling the pinch. It's a way to manage your money wisely and still help others.

Creating a **giving budget** is straightforward. Start by deciding on a portion of your income to allocate. This could be a percentage of your allowance or earnings from small jobs. For instance, you may give 5% of your allowance to charity. If you get $10 a week, that's 50 cents. It might not seem like much, but it adds up over time. Next, track your donations. Keep a record of how much you give and to whom. This helps you stay within your budget and see the impact of your contributions. You can use a notebook or a digital tool to record your donations.

There are **many ways to give** within a budget. Small, regular donations are a great start. Giving a little each month ensures you're consistently supporting your chosen cause. Fundraising efforts can also raise additional funds. Organize a lemonade stand, bake sale, or car wash to collect money for charity. This boosts your donations and gets others involved. Donating your time and skills is another valuable way to give. Volunteering doesn't cost money but can make a significant impact. Whether helping at a food bank or tutoring younger kids, your time is a precious gift.

Use tools like donation trackers and giving journals to keep track of your charitable activities. A donation tracker is a printable template or digital tool where you can record your contributions. Note the date, amount, and recipient. This helps you see how much you've given and ensures you stick to your budget. A giving journal is another excellent tool. It's a place to record your experiences and reflections on giving. Write about the causes you support, the people you help, and how it makes you feel. This keeps you organized and reminds you of the joy of giving.

Imagine using a spreadsheet to monitor your donations and volunteer hours. You create columns for the date, amount donated, hours volunteered, and the organization. Each time you give money or volunteer, you update the spreadsheet. Over time, you will see a detailed record of your charitable activities. This helps you stay within your budget and shows you the impact of your efforts. It's a simple yet powerful way to manage and reflect on your giving.

Budgeting for giving teaches financial responsibility and ensures regular contributions. It's about planning, tracking, and making thoughtful choices. Whether giving a small portion of your allowance, organizing fundraising events, or donating your time, every contribution counts. Use tools like donation trackers and giving journals to stay organized and see the impact of your efforts. With some planning, you can make a big difference while managing your money wisely.

## 7.13 REAL-LIFE STORIES OF YOUNG PHILANTHROPISTS: INSPIRING EXAMPLES

When we talk about giving back, it's always inspiring to hear about kids who have made significant differences in their communities. Take Abby Miller, for example. At just 12 years old, she used her musical talents to help others. She performed on the streets to raise funds for Taylor Love, a four-year-old battling neuroblastomas. Abby's efforts brought substantial donations, showing that even small acts can lead to significant impacts. Her story teaches us that age doesn't matter when making a difference. It's all about the heart and effort you put in.

Another great example is Olivia Bouler. At 11, she was heartbroken by the BP oil spill and its impact on birds. Instead of feeling helpless, she took action. Olivia offered her drawings to donors, raising over $200,000 for the National Audubon Society. Her story highlights the power of creativity and determination. Olivia faced the challenge of getting people to care about birds affected by the oil spill. But her passion and unique approach helped her overcome this obstacle. She showed that even in the face of disaster, one person can make a big difference.

Yet another inspiring story is that of Cameron Cohen. At 11, Cameron found himself in the hospital recovering from surgery. Instead of feeling sorry for himself, he created an iPhone drawing app called iSketch. He donated part of his earnings to buy entertainment items for hospitalized preteens. Cameron's journey was challenging. He had to learn coding and handle the business side of app development, all while dealing with his health issues. His persistence and creativity made life a bit brighter for other kids in the hospital.

There are many others, like Ryan Hreljac, who, at age 6, started fundraising to build wells in Africa after learning about the lack of clean water in many communities. Katie Stagliano, at age 9, started a vegetable garden to feed the hungry. Khloe Thompson, at age 8, began Khloe Kares, a nonprofit dedicated to helping homeless women and children. Hailey Fort, at age 9, began building mobile shelters for the homeless and started growing food to donate.

These young philanthropists faced many challenges. They had to find ways to make people care about their causes and raise funds. They had to balance their projects with school and other activities. But they didn't let these obstacles stop them. Instead, they used their creativity and persistence to overcome them. Their stories show that the rewards of giving go beyond money. They experienced personal growth, learned new skills, and made lasting impacts on their communities.

If these stories have sparked your interest, you might wonder how to start your **giving project**. The first step is to set a goal. Think about what you want to achieve and why it matters to you. Start small. You could aim to raise $50 for a local shelter or collect 100 books for a school library. Once you have a goal, take the first step. Talk to your family and friends about your idea. They can offer support and help you get started. Feel free to ask for help. Many people will be happy to support a good cause.

There are also opportunities for recognition and support for young philanthropists. Many programs and organizations offer awards and grants to kids making a difference. These can provide not just financial support but also motivation to keep going. Look for community support, too. Local businesses, schools, and organizations often have resources and networks that can help your project succeed. They can offer advice, donations, and even volunteers to help you reach your goals.

So, if you have an idea for giving back, go for it. Use these inspiring stories as motivation. Set your goals, take the first step, and seek support. You might be surprised at how much you can achieve and how rewarding the experience can be. Giving back isn't just about helping others. It's also about growing as a person and making lasting memories. And who knows? Your story could inspire people worldwide to embark on their giving project.

# CONCLUSION

Hey there, friends! We've come a long way together through this book. We've explored the exciting world of money and learned how to earn, save, spend, and even invest it. The goal of this book was simple. We wanted to help you and your family become money-smart. We wanted to ensure you have the tools and knowledge to make significant financial choices. Let's briefly review what we've covered and see what you can take away from all this.

First, we laid the foundation by understanding what money is and how it works. We looked at its history, from bartering to digital currency. We also talked about why it's so important to understand money. Knowing how to handle money helps you become independent, avoid debt, and make smart decisions.

Next, we dove into earning money. We explored different ways kids can earn money, like doing chores, starting small businesses, or making money online. We discussed creating chore charts, developing business ideas, and understanding the value of hard work.

We then moved on to saving and budgeting. We learned about the power of piggy banks and savings accounts. We also discussed setting financial goals and creating budgets to manage your allowance or earnings. Remember, saving money helps you prepare for the future and handle unexpected expenses.

When it came to spending, we discussed making wise choices. We examined comparing prices, avoiding impulse buys, and understanding the actual cost of owning things. We also learned about the value of spending on experiences rather than material items. Wise spending means getting the most out of your money.

Investing was another big topic. We learned that investing is like planting a seed that grows into a tree. We talked about stocks, bonds, and savings accounts. We also explored the magic of compound interest and how it helps your money grow faster. Investing is a way to make your money work for you.

We also covered digital financial tools like digital wallets, online banking, and budgeting apps. These tools make managing money easier and more convenient and help you keep track of your spending and savings.

Understanding credit and debt was another essential part of our journey. We learned what credit is and how to use it wisely. We also shared the risks of debt and how to avoid debt traps. Using credit responsibly helps you build a good credit score, which is vital for your financial future.

Finally, we explored philanthropy and financial responsibility. We learned about the joy of giving and how it helps make the world a better place. We talked about choosing causes to support, volunteering, and donating. Furthermore, we also looked at family-giving projects and budgeting for charitable contributions. Giving back is a beautiful way to positively impact your community.

So, what are the key takeaways from this book? First, understanding money is crucial. Knowing how to earn, save, spend, and invest helps you make smart financial choices. Second, saving and budgeting are essential skills. They prepare you for the future and help you achieve your financial goals. Third, wisely spending means getting the most value for your money. Fourth, investing helps your money grow. And finally, giving back brings joy and makes the world better.

But remember, learning about money continues. Keep practicing what you've learned. Keep earning, saving, spending, and investing wisely. Keep setting financial goals and working towards them. And keep finding ways to give back to your community. The more you practice, the better you'll manage your money.

Now, it's time for a call to action. Take what you've learned and put it into action. Start a chore chart, open a savings account, or set a financial goal. Try out a budgeting app or explore investment options. Most importantly, find a way to give back. Whether volunteering, donating, or organizing a family giving project, positively impact your community.

Remember, you're not alone on this journey. Your parents and I are here to help you along the way. Together, we can overcome financial ignorance and achieve mastery in personal finance. You've got this!

And here's a final inspirational note for you: Imagine a world where everyone understands money, kids and parents make smart financial choices, and communities come together to help each other. That's the world we're working towards. And it all starts with you. Your financial journey is just beginning. Keep learning, keep growing, and keep making a difference. The future is bright, and you're ready to shine!

# REFERENCES


Ducksters. (n.d.). *History of money*. Ducksters. https://www.ducksters.com/money/history_of_money.php

MoneySense. (n.d.). *How do banks work? | Banks explained for kids*. NatWest. https://natwest.mymoneysense.com/students/students-8-12/how-a-bank-works/

MyDoh. (n.d.). *Why kids and teens should start saving money early*. https://www.mydoh.ca/learn/money-101/money-basics/why-kids-and-teens-should-start-saving-money-early/

Webinar Strategy: Step-by-Step Guide to a Successful Webinar. https://www.getcontrast.io/learn/webinar-strategy

A Time of Reflection: Financial Goals to Set for 2024 | Workipedia by MyCareersFuture. https://content.mycareersfuture.gov.sg/time-of-reflection-financial-goals-set/

GoHenry. (n.d.). *The 8 best budgeting & money apps for kids & teens*. https://www.gohenry.com/uk/blog/financial-education/the-best-budgeting-apps-for-families

Joon App. (n.d.). *11 best chore apps for kids (for an easier family life)*. https://www.joonapp.io/post/chore-app-for-kids

Shopify. (2023). *The grown-up wisdom of 8 kid entrepreneurs*. https://www.shopify.com/blog/kid-entrepreneurs

HyperJar. (n.d.). *Guide to PayPal under 18: Age limits & alternatives*. https://hyperjar.com/blog/paypal-under-18-age-limits-and-alternatives

GoHenry. (n.d.). *How to make a business plan for kids (+ a free template)*. https://www.gohenry.com/us/blog/financial-education/how-to-make-a-business-plan-for-kids-a-free-template

HRIQ: Child Labor – Is It Okay? - Permian Basin Oil and Gas Magazine. https://pboilandgasmagazine.com/hriq-child-labor-is-it-okay/

Bank of America. (n.d.). *How to teach children the basics of budgeting*. Better Money Habits. https://bettermoneyhabits.bankofamerica.com/en/personal-banking/piggy-bank-for-kids

Bankrate. (n.d.). *How to open a savings account for a child*. https://www.bankrate.com/banking/savings/should-your-child-have-a-savings-account/

Money. (2024). Best high-yield savings accounts of 2024. Money.com. https://money.com/best-high-yield-savings-accounts/

Top Consumer Reviews. (2024). Best online savings accounts: Detailed reviews.

Top Consumer Reviews. https://www.topconsumerreviews.com/best-online-savings-accounts/detailed-reviews.php

Bing. (2024). Customer reviews and ratings for high-yield savings accounts 2024. Bing. https://www.bing.com/search

GoHenry. (n.d.). *The 8 best budgeting & money apps for kids & teens.* https://www.gohenry.com/uk/blog/financial-education/the-best-budgeting-apps-for-families.

Yoni, Author at Fiddlers-Inn Suites and Tzimmers in Tzfat. https://fiddlers-inn.net/author/yoni/

Blue Tree Savings. (n.d.). *How to teach your kids about: Emergency funds.* https://www.bluetreesavings.com/post/how-to-teach-your-kids-about-emergency-funds.

Consumer Financial Protection Bureau. (n.d.). *School-age children and shopping.* https://www.consumerfinance.gov/consumer-tools/money-as-you-grow/school-age-children-preteens/explore-shopping.

MyDoh. (n.d.). *How to help kids and teens avoid impulse buying.* https://www.mydoh.ca/learn/blog/lifestyle/how-to-help-kids-and-teens-avoid-impulse-buying/

How to Find 20 Percent Off a Number. https://www.ippude.com/how-to-find-20-percent-off-a-number/

Shop Smart, Not Hard: Save Big with Girls' School Uniforms on Sale – Faith Uniforms. https://faithuniforms.com/blogs/news/shop-smart-not-hard-save-big-with-girls-school-uniforms-on-sale

Bitcoin Scholarships: Opportunities for Students in the Digital Economy. https://bitlc.net/blog/bitcoin-scholarships-empowering-students-through-digital-currency-education

DEFI: HOW CRYPTOCURRENCIES DEMOCRATIZE FINANCIAL ACCESS. https://techshali.com/defi-how-cryptocurrencies-democratize-financial-access/

Navigating the Future: Unraveling the Dynamics of Digital Currencies. https://www.weal.asia/post/navigating-the-future-unraveling-the-dynamics-of-digital-currencies

What is Sustainable Bitcoin Mining?. https://blockchaininstitute.com/blog/sustainable-bitcoin-mining/

Banner Health. (n.d.). *Give your child experiences, not material things.* https://www.bannerhealth.com/healthcareblog/advise-me/give-your-child-experiences-not-material-things

Forbes. (2024). *Best debit cards for kids and teens of August 2024.* https://www.forbes.com/advisor/banking/best-debit-cards-kids-teens/

Bankrate. (n.d.). *Investing basics for kids: How to teach children to save and invest.* https://www.bankrate.com/investing/how-to-teach-kids-about-investing/

Mintos. (n.d.). *How do stocks work? A beginner's guide to the stock market.* https://www.mintos.com/blog/how-do-stocks-work/

Investopedia. (n.d.). *6 biggest bond risks.* https://www.investopedia.com/articles/bonds/08/bond-risks.asp

Investopedia. (n.d.). *The power of compound interest: Calculations and benefits.* https://www.investopedia.com/terms/c/compoundinterest.asp

Bloomberg. (2024, August 26). *How digital wallets like Apple Pay and Google Pay work.* https://www.bnnbloomberg.ca/business/international/2024/08/26/how-digital-wallets-like-apple-pay-and-google-pay-work/

AllCards. (n.d.). *The best money apps for kids and teens.* https://www.allcards.com/best-money-apps-for-kids-and-teens/

Bankaroo. (n.d.). *8 tips for keeping your kids safe when banking or shopping online.* https://bankaroo.com/8-tips-for-keeping-your-kids-safe-when-banking-or-shopping-online/

MakeUseOf. (n.d.). *10 interactive financial websites that teach kids money management skills.* https://www.makeuseof.com/tag/10-interactive-financial-websites-teach-kids-money-management-skills/

USAA. (n.d.). *Teaching your kids the basics about credit.* https://www.usaa.com/inet/wc/advice-family-kids-credit-basics

CNBC. (n.d.). *8 tips for parents to help their children build good credit early.* https://www.cnbc.com/select/steps-to-help-your-children-build-good-credit/

BMC Public Health. (2014). *Health effects of indebtedness: A systematic review.* https://bmcpublichealth.biomedcentral.com/articles/10.1186/1471-2458-14-489

Sallie Mae. (n.d.). *5 important credit card lessons for teens and young adults.* https://www.salliemae.com/blog/credit-card-lessons-for-young-adults/

Medium. (n.d.). *Teaching kids about philanthropy and giving: Why it matters.* https://medium.com/@myearlybean/teaching-kids-about-philanthropy-and-giving-why-it-matters-4a98b473e9c6

Arc Pathway. (n.d.). *The development of responsibility in the early years.* https://www.arcpathway.com/blog-article/the-development-of-responsibility-in-the-early-years.

Listverse. (2011, January 27). *10 great philanthropists who are kids.* https://listverse.com/2011/01/27/10-great-philanthropists-who-are-kids/

SignUpGenius. (n.d.). *50 community service ideas for families.* https://www.signupgenius.com/home/community-service-ideas-families.cfm